My Years as Chang Tsen

Two Wars, One Childhood

A Memoir

by

ANNABEL ANNUO LIU

My Years
as Chang Tsen

Two Wars, One Childhood

Also by Annabel Annuo Liu
(劉安諾)

哈囉，希兒薇亞！

乘著微笑的翅膀

風流與幽默

愛情的獵人

浮世情懷

人間多幽默

笑語人生

一杯半咖啡

for

Andrea, Doug, Clif, Tracy
&
Sylvia and Julia

CONTENTS

ONE

How This Book Was Born

I am an immigrant. I came to the United States from Taiwan on a freighter, with two suitcases and a hundred dollars—borrowed *by* my parents. More than half of the world's current population had not yet been born when I arrived in 1957 at age 22, fresh out of college. Like many of my peers, I went to graduate school, received a degree, got married and raised a family. Half a century went by. A few years into the new millennium, I retired and later became a widow. A stroke and subsequent pneumonia landed me across the continent, serving a life sentence without parole in a Pennsylvania senior living center.

For almost four years now I have been a solitary ethnic Chinese living among hundreds of American residents, most of whom are older than me. To be sure, I've always had a feeling of alienation, of living on the margins. But my isolation and the attendant cultural deprivation in an otherwise homogeneous institution have ironically accentuated the Chinese in me and made me *feel* more Chinese than ever.

Standing alone has intensified my sense of otherness even in my own family, with my American-born and bred children and grandchildren.

In my solitude during these twilight years, my distant past—the traumatic, war-torn childhood in China that I thought I had long put behind—has come to the fore, unbidden and more vivid than ever.

For Europeans, World War II began on September 1, 1939 when German soldiers marched across the border to Poland. For Americans, the same war did not start—not in a real sense, anyway—until Japan attacked Pearl Harbor on December 7, 1941. Few in the Western hemisphere are aware that Japan invaded Manchuria, the northeastern part of China, in 1931—ten years before Pearl Harbor. This invasion was succeeded by a series of so-called incidents until the Second Sino-Japanese War—the largest Asian war of the twentieth century—officially started on July 7, 1937. Thus, Japan and China had already been at war for four full years before Pearl Harbor, and remained at war until Japan surrendered four years later. An estimated 20 million Chinese perished, roughly twice the combined population of New York City and Washington, D.C.

In short, China was in great turmoil throughout my childhood. During twelve of the first fourteen years of my life, my native country fought two major wars. After the first (the eight-year Sino-Japanese War), the second one (the Chinese civil war) began without any pause to allow the country to recover from the ravages of Japanese aggression. An additional 2.5 million lives were lost by the time the civil war ended. The victorious Communists established the People's Republic of China on October 1, 1949, and Mao Zedong proclaimed in Tiananmen Square: "We Chinese have stood up in the world."

Nobody could have predicted the subsequent toll of what Mao named "politics with bloodshed." Thirty years of unremitting so-called political movements, purges, and ignorant, wrong-headed policies plunged the country into one catastrophe after another, culminating in Mao's masterpiece, the most violent, most heinous upheaval of all time—the Great Cultural Revolution. All told, an estimated 77 million Chinese died as a result of his policies and actions—nearly four times the number slaughtered by the Japanese.

In total, 100 million Chinese—equivalent to one-third of the current U.S. population—were killed during the first 40 years of my life, the bloodiest chapter of all human history.

This book tells the story of one precarious yet remarkably fortunate life—my life——against this horrendous tapestry.

By profession I'm a bilingual writer. As a free-lancer, I wrote feature stories, in-depth interviews, and occasional guest columns for the *Ames Daily Tribune* and the *Des Moines Register* for ten years, then switched to literary essays and short fiction in Chinese, including a 60,000-word novella. My twenty-year Chinese-writing endeavor resulted in the publication of eight books.

I have always found it regrettable that my children, both illiterate in Chinese, cannot read what I wrote in Chinese and consequently don't know me as well as many of my Chinese readers. In my retirement, I have begun dabbling in poetry and have embarked on a memoir of sorts, both in English.

While doing so I realized that in my 20-year Chinese writing career, I touched upon my life in bits and pieces, but never made a serious effort to make sense of it, let alone write about it in a systematic way.

This book covers the first fourteen years of my life, my most formative years. Like a tattoo upon my soul, the years of 1941-45—when I was six to ten living under Japanese occupation and escaping and hiding from the Japanese military police—left indelible emotional scars plus myriad adverse health effects, including severe allergies, an enlarged heart and defective valves, with which I struggle to this day. During the ensuing civil war, there was an all-too-brief period when our family lived in relative peace. It was also an eventful time I recall with fondness and regret. Shortly before the Communist victory in the civil war, we fled across the Taiwan Strait to a remote little island, known at the time as Formosa. The epilogue of this book depicts the aftermath— how our family was torn apart by the Communist regime brought on by the two wars.

In essence, we were nothing but hapless, insignificant pawns tossed by inexorable political currents against a gigantic historical backdrop. Perhaps the story I tell in this book is only extraordinary in the sense that some of us survived at all. But it's a story I know and feel compelled to tell.

Two

Born in the Shadow of War

1935-1939

I was 30 years old, expecting my second child, when I learned the circumstances of my own birth.

During the summer of 1965, my parents arrived in the States from Saigon where they had spent two years. My father, who enjoyed a successful career building up Taiwan's fisheries industry, had been in Saigon as a fisheries consultant. They visited my brother Charley, sister Lining, and cousins Paul and Cecilia, all on the East Coast. Finally they came to visit me in Iowa. It had been eight years since I had seen them last, when I left home to come to this country in 1957.

In that time, I had transformed—from a sheltered 22-year old never allowed out of the house except for school, to a young married woman with one child and another prominently showing. My parents had come from Cousin Paul's New York City apartment, where Paul and his wife Francene had hastened to paint their chipped and cratered bathroom sink white in preparation for my parents' arrival; and here I was, living in a shiny, new four-bedroom house.

For once I detected my father regarding me with something that I was unfamiliar with—something akin to approval. Perhaps that was what motivated him to talk to me as one adult to another—again something I was unfamiliar with, since we had talked only twice in all the years we spent under one roof, and certainly never as one adult to another.

It was a fine afternoon, not too hot. My husband Sam had left after lunch to go back to work, and our daughter Andrea and my mother were napping upstairs. I was wiping the stove, my back to my father at the kitchen table, as his words rose above the joint hum of the dishwasher and central air conditioner...

"Shortly after your brother was born," he began, "your mother was pregnant again and determined to have an abortion."

My brother had arrived two months earlier than expected. He was "as small as a mouse" and wasn't given much chance for survival. And his wet nurse turned out to have beriberi. So it had been a very traumatic time.

"I was against the whole idea, of course," my father continued, "but you know how stubborn your mother can be. She even got the woman professor at her medical school to perform the operation.

"On the appointed day I waited outside the operating room. I could hear the clinking of the metal utensils and the low voices of the doctor and nurses inside. Suddenly I heard your mother moan. It was not loud, but distinct, as if she were in great pain that she was trying her best to suppress but couldn't.

"We all know your mother is stoic, extremely so. When she was in labor before your brother was born, she never screamed or cursed like all the other women. Afterward the nurses couldn't stop talking about how brave she was. Now she was moaning and groaning. My scalp tingled when I heard her. I thought she was going to die. Abortion was illegal. I could go to jail and lose my attorney's license.

"I don't know how long the ordeal lasted, but when the doctor came out of the room to tell me it went well, I found I had been in a cold sweat. I had never been so scared in my whole life. But would you believe it? After she woke up, she didn't even remember any moaning at all. She assured me she had general anesthesia and suffered no pain."

He paused.

"Despite what she said, more than a year later, when she was pregnant again and wanted to go through the same procedure, I put my foot down," he said. "That was why you were born."

I was speechless—his confession was so unexpected, so uncharacteristically candid. Our communication pattern had been set since I was a tot—a one-way street. He issued his edict or verdict. This time was no exception. He talked; I listened.

My father's stories always had a moral to them. In this case it was obvious: I should be grateful to him for saving my life. But the way I saw it, I owed my existence to my mother's moans under anesthesia.

One can't have a beginning more tenuous and inauspicious than that.

I was two years old when the Imperial Japanese Army opened fire on Marco Polo Bridge near Beijing, China, sparking The Second Sino-Japanese War, the largest Asian war of the twentieth century. I was ten when the U.S. dropped two atomic bombs on Japan, bringing the war to an end.

I lived with the reality of war for eight out of the first ten years of my life, six of them in Japanese-occupied Shanghai. During those eight years, 1937-45, an estimated 20-million Chinese lost their lives, but my family survived by a hairsbreadth.

Some years ago, I read that on New Year's Eve, Japanese Buddhist temples ring bells 108 times to commemorate Japan's hardships. *Japan's hardships!* I felt as if someone had punched me in the chest with an iron fist. What about China's hardships, especially those caused by Japan? How many times should we ring *our* bells?

My parents were married in Shanghai in September 1931. Both were in their last year of school—he in law, she, medicine. That year, the new Republic turned 20 years old and Japan invaded China, taking control of Manchuria in the north—all 200,000 square kilometers of its land and rich resources—as the prelude to the Second Sino-Japanese War. After my father graduated from law school a year later, he worked as an attorney and taught law part-time at his alma mater, Dongwu University in Shanghai. The Americans had their roaring '20s. For my parents as wealthy newlyweds in the cosmopolitan city of Shanghai far from Manchuria, life in the early '30s was also carefree and glamorous, full of movies, dancing, mahjongg, horse racing, and even dog racing. My father, gregarious by nature, thrived. I don't think my mother knew how to dance or play mahjongg before she met him, but she was a quick study and caught up with him.

My father, Liu Yongchio, as a young man. Both photos were taken by his friend, Wu Yinxian, who later became one of the leading photographers of the Communist party.

My father signed his name the French way, Lieou, because his elder brother was educated in France.

My brother was born in 1932 in the midst of the good life. They called him Charley, the only one of their children to be given an English name. I was born in 1935—a tumultuous year in Chinese history. I was named Annuo.

By then, a little uneasiness had crept into my parents' comfortable and cosmopolitan life. Much like rodents that seem to possess an extrasensory skill to detect a coming seismic event, my parents and their friends felt the war building.

The establishment of the Republic of China in 1911 ended one of the most humiliating periods in Chinese history—the second half of the nineteenth century. Under the corrupt and impotent Qing Dynasty, China suffered a string of military defeats, including the two Opium Wars with the British Empire when Hong Kong was ceded and the import of opium was legitimized against our will; the First Sino-Japanese War, when Taiwan was lost and Korea became a colony of Japan instead of a vassal state of China; and finally the Boxer Rebellion, which resulted in eight nations' troops occupying and plundering the Chinese capital, Beijing. In each of these wars, huge amounts of war reparations had to be paid to the victors.

Years later, when I was in high school in Taiwan, my history teacher characterized that part of our past as *yibu xueleishi*, a volume of history of blood and tears. Our teacher's voice grew low and heavy, the classroom hushed, and we all hung our heads in shame.

In 1935, the year I was born, the end of 5,000 years of imperial dynasties had been achieved a mere 24 years before, and democracy was still on shaky ground. In addition to rampant warlords and a deeply ingrained dynastic tradition, the government had Japan to contend with. Japan did not stop with conquering Manchuria; it continually instigated *incidents*, their euphemism for invasions. With each incident, China lost more territory.

What's more, the central government, controlled by the Nationalist party, which founded the Republic, had yet another pressing problem on its hands: the increasingly popular Communists. With Mao Zedong as their leader, the Chinese Communists, like their Russian comrades in 1917, set their sights on overturning the government. Unsurprisingly, their idea didn't sit well with the Nationalists, led by Chiang Kai-shek. The upshot was that in 1934-35 Mao and his followers made a long trek—known historically as the Long March—to remote, poverty-stricken Yan'an of Shaanxi province, where they were too far away and isolated to be reached by the power of the central government.

At that critical juncture, the Chinese population could be divided roughly into three groups. The overwhelming majority might be characterized as obedient citizens, to use a Chinese expression. They did what their forebears had done for thousands of years. They were apolitical, minded their own business, and did whatever it took to survive or to prosper, regardless of who was in power.

The other two groups were determined to *jiuguo*—save our country—but differed in their approach. One group opted to work for the Nationalists. The last group of intrepid souls, believing only a Communist revolution could thoroughly change the country, took the most daring option—and my parents knew some of them.

One of their numerous mahjongg and dancing friends, a third-rate actress by the name of Lan Ping, left Shanghai for the Communist safe haven Yan'an and changed her name to Jiang Qing. She married Mao Zedong and became known as Madame Mao—of "Gang of Four" fame, or I should say, notoriety.

(If politics makes strange bedfellows, mahjongg certainly makes stranger ones. My father spent his childhood and adolescent years playing mahjongg to provide company for his early widowed mother. Over the years, he, and by association, my mother, socialized with all kinds of characters they called friends simply because they played mahjongg together. I grew up devoid of any inclination to play mahjongg, and by extension, bridge or any other time-consuming game.)

Another Communist was my father's best friend Wu Yinxian, a photographer with an artistic bent. He sold his photo studio and also took off for Yan'an.

In those days, it was life-threatening to openly be a Communist or Communist sympathizer. Wu didn't divulge his intentions, not even to my father. Before he left Shanghai, however, he did make a date with my father to spend his last night there with him, for what the Chinese poetically call *lianchuang yehua*—to link beds together for a night's conversation.

The journey Wu was about to take was a long and arduous one, and extraordinarily perilous. He probably wished to explain how he had come to this most crucial decision of his life, hoping to persuade my father to follow him. Perhaps there were things he wanted my father to do in case something happened to him. As luck would have it, that night my father came down with a 24-hour flu. He was violently sick and ran a high fever. Although Wu came and spent the night, my father was in no shape to talk or listen.

When my father later discovered Wu's destination, he thought it was remarkably lucky that he was sick that night. Otherwise he might have been persuaded, and our lives would have been drastically different.

As it turned out, my father was soon recruited by the Nationalists, and left Shanghai and his young family to go to Guiyang, the capital of Guizhou province, to serve as the personal secretary of Wu Zhongxin, governor of Guizhou. Wu was an early revolutionary who had helped to bring forth the Republic and was a trusted deputy and comrade of Chiang Kai-shek.

Unwittingly, my father and his photographer friend found themselves on the opposite sides of the political spectrum. Their paths never crossed again.

In my father's old age I had a chance to ask him why he had abandoned his comfortable life in Shanghai for an uncertain future in the hinterland. Going from Shanghai to Guizhou almost amounted to self-exile. What's more, he had been making 800 yuan a month in Shanghai, a fabulous sum at that time. Despite the fact that neither of my parents could ever be accused of being thrifty, they couldn't spend it all. In contrast, a government job paid next to nothing.

He said that, as an attorney in the French Concession, his work of mainly defending petty criminals was too easy and boring. And their life in Shanghai was getting rather decadent. He wanted to do something meaningful for a change. Perhaps the war handed a purpose in life to this *playboy*, as his elder brother, the scholar of the family, deridingly labeled him.

I was a few weeks old when my father left for Guizhou, and my brother was not quite three. Guizhou, an impoverished and backward province largely inhabited by a minority called *Miaos*, was not exactly a hospitable place for a young family from cosmopolitan Shanghai. Before my father left, he arranged to have my mother and two children move to Yangzhou, his hometown in Jiangsu province, to live with his family. With the war imminent, he thought we would be safer in Yangzhou.

But his idea didn't work out well. His widowed mother and his sisters treated my mother with something worse than a cold shoulder. In a little more than a year, while

Photos of Annuo

My brother Charley and me

he was still far away in Guizhou, my mother, unhappy in Yangzhou, became sick with ulcers. She took my brother and me back to Shanghai—just in time for another Japanese *incident.* This particular one, however, lasted more than three months, involved nearly one million troops, and went down in history as the Battle of Shanghai, the first and one of the largest, most fiercely fought, and bloodiest battles of the entire war.

They fought inch by inch on the beaches of the Jiangsu coast, where the Japanese made amphibious landings. They fought from house to house, in outlying towns and metropolitan Shanghai. The Chinese had only small caliber weapons, no cannons or tanks. They were outgunned by Japan's far superior military might, but not outnumbered. Battalions of Chinese soldiers were slaughtered, and new battalions were sent in.

Frustrated and angered by the unexpectedly stiff resistance, the Japanese introduced a new form of warfare—deliberate mass murder of civilians by bombing metropolitan Shanghai, a city of 3.5 million. Terrified refugees flooded the French Concession and the International Settlement, and gates had to be closed against the overflowing refugees.

Concessions in China were born from the unequal treaties that China was forced to sign with various foreign powers, in which enclaves in Chinese cities were conceded to respective foreign powers, who could occupy and enjoy sovereignty in the specified area. Unbound by Chinese laws, they had their own police, and in some cases, even a small military force. In essence, each concession was a miniature country within country. Shanghai had two—the French Concession where my parents lived and the International Settlement (the joint concessions of the United Kingdom, the United States, and Japan).

During the Battle of Shanghai when Japan engaged in massive bombing of the city, only the French Concession and the International Settlement were safe, because Japan was not at war with those three Western countries at the time.

More than 70 years later, sitting in the security of my apartment in the senior living center in Pennsylvania, I sobbed as I saw on the Internet the images of desperate refugees shut out by the gates of the concessions, and a photo titled "Bloody Saturday," of a burned, terrified, bawling baby, the lone survivor in the bombed wreckage of Shanghai South Railway Station on August 28, 1937.

My family was lucky. We were protected from bombing and fighting because we were living in the French Concession throughout the carnage. In fact, my mother went to a hospital in the French Concession and volunteered her services, helping treat the wounded. Ironically, from the slaughter came the only opportunity for my mother to practice medicine in her life. My brother, who was five at the time, remembers people rushing to the hospital to give blood, and Boy Scouts crawling in the streets to deliver supplies to the front lines.

After Shanghai fell, we set off immediately for Guizhou to join our father. It had been two years since we had seen him last. By then, my father's superior, the man who recruited him, Wu Zhongxin, had left for a new position, and another Wu, by the name of Wu Dingchang, had taken over as provincial governor, and made my father the magistrate of Pingba county.

Because of the war, we had to take a circuitous sea route. From Shanghai we embarked on the steamship "The Japanese Empress" which took us to Hong Kong. In those days, a passenger liner was not unlike a present-day cruise ship. There we switched to a small motorboat to Guangzhou, the capital of

Guangdong province. A different motorboat took us west on Xijiang (West River), to Liuzhou in Guangxi province. From there we took a bus to Guiyang where our father waited for us. We then all boarded a bus for Pingba.

My brother Charley was only five years old at the time. It absolutely amazes me that now, almost 80 years old, he can still recall the entire route and the different modes of transportation we took during the trip. He proudly ticked off the above itinerary to me but neglected to mention that he would become horribly seasick the moment our ship or boat started and remained so until it stopped. I got that fact from a reliable source and was able to confirm his seasickness later in our travels together. I, on the contrary, never suffered seasickness. I was only two and have no memory of this, but the same reliable source told me that I practically shone on the ship, singing and dancing at the prompting of passengers and crew—the life of the party.

My memory began sometime after we arrived in Pingba. Memory is such a peculiar, selective process. One has no control over what will firmly imprint itself in the mind and remain decades later, and what will be erased as if it had never happened.

My earliest memory is vague, visual. I was playing in the garden. The sun was beating unmercifully on me, and I demanded to be changed into clothes "one hundred times thinner" than what I had on. I'm sure I had no concept of what it meant; I was merely repeating someone else's words that had impressed me.

At bedtime, my mother used to tell me a story. In fact, each time she told the same story of mice stealing pancakes, a story, I suspect, she made up. From our stay with my father's family in Yangzhou, I had grown fond of a kind of savory pancake with meat and vegetable filling called Yangzhou *lan-mian shaobing*—*lanmian* meaning soft dough—a specialty of Yangzhou. When my mother told me the story about mice stealing pancakes, I assumed it was this kind of pancakes the mice had designs on. I never tired of hearing the story, but never managed to find out what happened to the mice or the pancakes before falling fast asleep each time.

As I mentioned before, Guizhou was known for having a large population of a minority people—the Miaos. I was fascinated by the servants' talk that women in the Miao tribe didn't wear underpants inside their blue and white batik costumes. Unfortunately, I lacked the courage to peek when we saw them at open-air markets, so could not prove whether or not the story was true.

We lived in the magistrate's official residence. It sounded grand but it was just a hodgepodge of buildings, with the county offices in front, including the county jail where prisoners were held. We lived in the back, at the bottom of the U-shaped quarters, while the deputy and chief of staff's families occupied the uprising arms of the U.

Once my brother discovered that executions (by beheading) were to be held on the small square outside our building. Guizhou was a poor province, abundant with bandits. They were sometimes called *tufei*, land pirates, because they often resorted to kidnapping, in addition to pillaging and killing. My brother discovered that some captured bandits were to be executed the next morning. We got up early, my brother led the way, and we sneaked out the side door to watch. Not knowing executions were held during predawn hours, we arrived too late. The heads were already displayed on the poles. He saw the blood and the painful grimaces on those faces, but I don't remember seeing anything. When our father found out later what we had done, he was so angry that my brother nearly suffered a spanking.

Another time my brother and I got into a great quantity of delicious dried chestnuts and surreptitiously gorged on them to the extent of suffering from severe diarrhea. It was a cold winter night, and we only had one thermos of hot water in the house. None of this remotely amused our mother.

For some reasons I still have a photo of our family taken in Guizhou before my sister was born—our family plus a little boy. In the photo, my arm is draped affectionately around the little boy's shoulder. He was my father's deputy's son and had the habit of calling me his *Lao Po* (old woman). His family lived in sepa-

Back row (from left): My father, Liu Yongchio, and my mother, Dai Shangying. Front row (from left): Me, my father's deputy's son, and my brother Charley.

rate quarters in the same residence; the three of us were said to be inseparable, but I only remember one thing. On the day my sister was born, we three were fighting for a chance to peep through the keyhole of my parents' room. I didn't see a thing, but was extremely excited all the same.

All in all, our two years in Guizhou were an interesting adventure for my brother and me. But what was it like for our mother? Leaving Shanghai for Guizhou was akin to leaving New York City for a Montana log cabin sans running water and electricity. My father was the up-and-coming young magistrate, involved in his work, but my mother was confined to the magistrate's residence, with nothing to do except play mahjongg with employees' wives.

What was worse, she received news that her father died after a brief illness. My mother had been exceptionally close to her father. When she was a child, her feet had been bound according to the custom of the time—an extremely painful and debilitating process. After she spent more than a week crying and pleading with her father, he allowed her to be the first female in the family to unbind her feet. Later he was the one who gave her permission to go to school—another first—freeing her from the bondage of illiteracy. And he was also the one who supported her desire to attend a missionary high school and then to go all the way to Shanghai to study medicine—an unheard-of undertaking for a young woman at that time. But now, with a baby due, the great distance between Guizhou and Anhui (the province my mother was from), and most important of all, the war, it was impossible for her to go home for his funeral. In fact, because of the war, she never went home again.

The last time she saw her father was after we left Yangzhou on our way back to Shanghai, just before the Battle of Shanghai. My brother, almost five at the time, still remembers our maternal grandfather's room, his bed, and the drawers on the headboard where he kept sweets. He remembers how our grandfather smiled when he brought out the treats for us. None of us, including my mother, realized that visit would be the last time we would ever see him or my mother's home. For me, it was the only time.

I recently Googled my father in Chinese and discovered a story about his experience as a magistrate in Pingba that I never knew. At that time, Guizhou farmers were growing opium as their principal crop. The Nationalist government's Military Committee issued a decree banning the growing of opium. All existing opium plantings were to be dug up and taken out immediately.

The governor of Guizhou, Wu Dingchang, later wrote in his memoir about the episode. He said that my father weighed the problem all night. He went to Guiyang, the capital, to see Wu and said, "Our farmers worked hard all year, and opium is their only source of income. I have decided to require them to take out only those plants within one *li* (Chinese mile) of both sides of the highway, to allow them to harvest the opium in the rest of their fields, and to make sure they plant something else next season. For not fully complying with the decree, I will take the responsibility and punishment."

Wu wrote that he thought for a minute, jumped up, and pounded his fist hard on the desk: "Good magistrate! You are putting the farmers' welfare ahead of yourself. I will not punish you. Go back and continue your good work." The story later was repeated all over Guizhou as an example of Wu Dingchang and my father's caring administrative style. (At that time, another governor could easily have had my father executed for openly disobeying the Military Committee's decree.)

We lived in Pingba for less than two years. In early 1939 my sister was born. A few months later, we were on our way back to Shanghai.

The war had not been going well for China. After the fall of Shanghai, our capital Nanking was soon lost, in what became known as the Massacre of Nanking or the Rape of Nanking. In a six-week period, 200,000 females of all ages were raped, yet another Japanese tactic to break the Chinese will to resist.

(By some estimates, the dead in the Nanking massacre totaled 300,000.) The Western powers were shocked by the Japanese behavior but chose to do nothing. Refusing to surrender, Chiang Kai-shek retreated to the interior of China to continue the fight. Chongqing, the capital of Sichuan province, became the nation's new wartime capital.

A family photo taken shortly before we left Guizhou for Shanghai. Back row (from left): My father's younger brother-in-law, my father, and my mother holding my infant sister, Lining. Front row, my brother Charley and me, Annuo. We were heading back to war and the Japanese-occupied zone. For six years, no more photos were taken of any of us except for identification cards.

The brutality of the Japanese infuriated many Chinese, including my father. In Guizhou he had met Han Deqin, the governor of my father's home province of Jiangsu and commander of the Shandong and Jiangsu War zone. Instead of staying in Guizhou, which was away from the war, my father chose to go to Jiangsu to fight the Japanese directly under Commander

Han. The family, of course, would be better off near our relatives in Shanghai.

The Chinese like to tout the tradition of *sidai tongtang*—four generations under the same roof. In the case of our family, both sides had only three generations under the same roof. The war uprooted the matriarchs and scattered my parents' siblings and their children all over the country. On my father's side, Nainai, my paternal grandmother, and Wu Niangniang, my father's older sister and closest sibling—both treated my mother rather shabbily—both had to abandon our ancestral home in Yangzhou and flee to Shanghai to escape the Japanese. Nainai stayed with my father's older brother, San Bobo. Wu Niangniang, having lost her husband to tuberculosis, remarried in Shanghai.

On my mother's side, the matriarch was Wainainai, my newly widowed maternal grandmother. "Wai" means *outside*, the Chinese way of denoting that mother came from another family. Wainainai also had to abandon the ancestral home in Hefei, Anhui, and went to live in the hinterland of Lanzhou, Gansu, with my third maternal uncle San Jiu, whom I've never met. My mother probably didn't know where her other three surviving brothers were. Her closest sibling was her younger sister, whom we called Yiniang, or maternal aunt; Yiniang was married and lived in Shanghai.

We left Pingba by bus for Guiyang, and from there, again by bus, to Kunming in Yunnan province. At one stop, my mother, holding my baby sister, lost her balance while dismounting from the bus and fell—the first of many falls in her life, from the foot binding in childhood that permanently deformed her feet. Rather than risk injuring the baby, she used her head to break the fall and suffered a serious head injury. I remember she looked like a wounded soldier afterward, with her head wrapped in bandages stained by blood. Decades later I wondered if the Alzheimer's disease that she suffered in her old age could be traced back to that severe blow to the head.

In all their years together, I only heard my father praise my mother for two things: this incident, and the fact that she could remember which item was in which suitcase when they needed it. Apparently that was all that impressed him about her.

We had to wait in Kunming for three months for our visas to travel through Vietnam to return to Shanghai. The war had blocked the land route, which would have been more direct. I remember the frequent Japanese bombing raids. There were no bomb shelters. Many times we had to run out of the city to hide in the woods. To assuage hunger afterward, the only food we could buy were candied hawthorn apples on a stick.

From Kunming we went by train to Laojie at the border on the way to Hanoi and Haiphong in Vietnam. While we were sitting in the train in Laojie waiting for it to depart, a man, obviously an experienced traveler in the area, warned our father about the pickpockets—he called them "three hands." As he was talking, the train began to move, and someone from outside the window—leisurely, almost good naturedly—snatched his hat. The surprise and embarrassment on the face of that suddenly hatless gentleman was something to behold.

In Haiphong we boarded a steamship to Hong Kong. I don't remember getting off the ship in Hong Kong but do have a vivid impression of the beautiful lights and the small tin of animal crackers given to my brother and me by our parents' friends.

We arrived in Shanghai one afternoon, months after setting out on the journey. On seeing the famous Bund, my mother reminded me of a story of two years before when we left Shanghai. I hadn't been able to contain my excitement and hollered, "Look, Muma, lots and lots of coffee!" Indeed, the color of water of Huangpu River was like coffee with milk.

Two years had gone by; I had forgotten what coffee looked like. Shanghai and my parents had changed, too. Only the color of Huangpu River remained the same.

THREE

My First Lesson of War

1939-1941

Once back in Shanghai, my father lost no time in departing for his new and deadly work in northern Jiangsu. I have absolutely no memory of his leaving, but in his old age he did, for once, tell me the following:

"One afternoon I asked your mother how much money we had in the house. She took out her purse, searched in the drawers and gave it all to me. I bade her not to go out and work and instructed her to borrow money from relatives when necessary. She tried to hand me the baby—'Just hold her for a little while.' I knew if I did, it would be hard for me to leave. So I went straight out the front door without ever looking back."

Yes, that was what a patriotic young man had to do, but what about his wife and three small children? How would they survive? For a while we subsisted on cornmeal, the cheapest food one could buy. No matter what one did to disguise or enhance it, it was the same coarse and taste-less cornmeal. I remember hating that stuff and refusing to eat it, and hence was stuck ever afterward with the label of a picky eater.

Eating cornmeal is all I remember about my father's absence at the time. How did my mother feel when my father left to fight? Even in her old age she never said one word about it. At 32, married eight years, she was left facing a future fraught with danger, with three small children, the youngest not yet a year old. She could count on no help from her husband. In fact, she had no way of knowing whether he was dead or alive...

What a contrast between then and now, she probably thought. Years later on the eve of our departure from the Chinese mainland for Taiwan, I happened to glimpse my parents' engagement photo taken by my father's photographer friend Wu Yinxian, who joined the Communists. Wu had posed my parents in profile, both wearing the fashionable black-framed round glasses of the time, looking ahead in unison, with intent, serious expressions.

I was not yet fourteen, but somehow it was heartbreaking to see my parents so young, so full of hope for the future, and so sure of their happiness.

Now this.

Before long my mother had to borrow money for the first time in her life. The natural and only choice was the person closest to her—her younger sister, our aunt Yiniang, who had followed her to Shanghai, graduated from Fudan University and married my father's good friend and class-mate, whom we called simply Shushu, younger paternal uncle. They had three children at the time: two girls and one boy.

Yiniang, of course, had to ask her husband, who immediately went to their bedroom, came out with a handful of cash, and apologized, "I know it's not much, but this is all of our children's New Year's red envelope money."

It is the custom that on Chinese New Year's Eve, grandparents, parents and other older relatives give children money in cash in red envelopes, to be put under their pillows for the night, for health, good luck, prosperity, and long life.

Throughout the Chinese New Year celebration, for 10 to 15 days, it is also the custom for people to go to their relatives' and friends' houses to *beinian*, to wish them a prosperous New Year. Visitors are armed

My mother's younger sister, Yiniang, and her husband, Shushu, with their two older children.

with red envelopes containing cash for the children of each house. In those days, depending on how many relatives and friends one's parents had, a child could expect to harvest a fairly decent sum of money. However, typically the kids had to turn it over to their parents for safekeeping, which meant they would never see it again. I, for one, received numerous red envelopes in my childhood and never got to spend a penny.

Shushu's mention of their children's red-envelope money implied we were robbing their little ones' piggybank. Besides, there wouldn't be any more red-envelope money until next year. He was tactfully closing the door on lending us more money.

One could hardly blame him. He was making good money as an attorney, but as the eldest son in his family, he had to support his parents and his large extended family, in addition to his wife and children. My father might be away for years, or might not ever return. How could we expect Shushu to take on the extra burden of supporting his sister-in-law and three children?

My father would never admit it, but he really did not wish my mother to work. Before they were married, he had promised my mother's father that he would allow her to practice medicine, the goal of her years of hard work in defiance of the tradition that kept women illiterate and dependent on their husbands. Now he had the best reason to break his promise: Because he was fighting underground, it would be safer for his family to keep a low profile in Japanese-occupied Shanghai. As it happened, however, he was away for six years. His idea of borrowing from relatives failed from the beginning. My mother had no choice but to take the risk of finding employment. Other than that short stint as a volunteer in a French Concession hospital during the Battle of Shanghai, my mother had been out of the medical field for seven years. Practicing medicine, in any case, would be too risky. Luckily with her connections she was able to obtain work at a drug company, CBC Pharmaceuticals.

Nowadays when I go to doctors' offices, I can often spot good-looking young women or men from pharmaceutical companies with bulging briefcases. Their job is to persuade doctors to try their new products. I look at them with a pang in my heart. My mother supported us for almost six years doing just that.

After we returned to Shanghai from Guizhou, we rented the fourth floor of a residence at 474 Avenue Lafayette in the French Concession, from an attorney named Yu Zhongluo. It was the same apartment my father had lived in as a student attending Dongwu University. In fact, my brother Charley was born at that address. When my father started working, they moved to better dwellings. Now that my father had gone away to join the Resistance, austerity was in order. We were back on Yu's fourth floor again. Because of the long friendly association, Charley always called Yu Zhongluo "Yu Ganye." For want of a better term, *Ganye* may be translated as *godfather* with no religious connotations. *Gan* literally means "dry," denoting no blood relations.

My brother and I were enrolled in the nearby elementary school with a French name. I was four, in the kindergarten class.

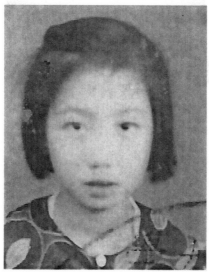

This is probably a photo for kindergarten registration.

The Occasion

In my memories
a small fuchsia dress
reposes apart forever new
forever ravishing like
a poppy in full bloom

rosy-hued organza
puff sleeves skirt rippling
like a lotus leaf in breeze
draped over my bedroom chair
each night before sleep I run
my hand gently over its delicate fabric
waiting, waiting for *the occasion*—
the last day of school

hands folded on my knees
I wait to be called
to the podium for the prizes
wooden pencil boxes
covers painted with Snow White
and the seven dwarfs
Dorothy of the Wizard of Oz
Alice in Wonderland…

and what treasures they hold—
slim sharpened pencils
clock-shaped eraser
gleaming sharpener
wine-colored celluloid ruler
each nestling in its perfect slot

my turn never comes
instead, a verdict
in bold red letters awaits
Repeat kindergarten

vision blurred by the merciless sun
the new dress like shards
of broken glass on my back
I walk home in a daze

at the sight of Mother
coming down stairs the tears
I struggled to hold
burst out in torrent
pushing away her hands
with all my might I hug
the end post of the banister
and bawl and bawl

I never wore
that dress
again.

June 2005
Revised July 2007

Years later my mother told me that because I spoke
mainly the Guizhou dialect learned from the servants,
she enrolled me half a year early in kindergarten to give
me time to learn the Shanghai dialect. Actually I learned
Shanghainese in a very short time, but still I was considered too young, so her arrangement with the school stood.

Nobody thought of informing me of the decision or the reason. I believe my mother meant well. She probably reasoned, "She's too little to know the difference. Besides, a new dress should cheer her up." In reality it served to deepen my shame.

The Yu family owned the four-story house we lived in. They occupied the three lower levels; we lived on the fourth floor and shared their kitchen on the first. My brother and I played with their kids regularly.

Their family was much more traditional than ours. They kept one room for worshiping ancestors. Drawn by the scent of burning incense one day, I took one stick and touched it on a box of matches perched on a glass ashtray with all the heads up and out. "BOOM"! Instantly my hair and eyebrows were gone, and hand, face and neck singed. Fortunately, my mother was home; she rushed downstairs to tend my wounds.

In addition to the pain, I must have been quite a sight. For many months kids on the street called me "African." Summer on the fourth floor was hot and humid. Mother used a syringe to draw out the perspiration inside the blisters on my face. She did the blisters one by one, patiently and carefully. Thanks to her, I have no scars on my face.

Yu Ganye had five children, two girls, two boys, then another girl my age with whom I played but no longer remember. The only one I remember is their second daughter Yu Zhonghe. She was in high school, a quiet, scholarly girl, but very beautiful, and I admired everything about her. Her given name Zhonghe literally means *peace in China*. Years later when I saw Ingmar Bergman's movie "The Virgin Spring," I thought of her. I wrote my very first poem in English about her.

The Dead

Daily I check my mirror
for hints of dowager's hump
my grandchild wants to know
why on my chin
this big fold

ancient in her eyes
I have memories
that take me back
to that far, faraway land
my childhood

I was five
admiring our neighbor so wise
so gentle so beautiful
shoulder-length raven hair
shimmering under the lamp
clasped with a tortoise barrette
on the lapel of her qipao
a jaunty fountain pen

one night her mother came
tears scalding her cheeks
crumpled note in hand
my idol had left with friends
to join the Red Army
to save our country
from the invading enemy

hope and zeal all
came to naught
when they were caught
by Japanese soldiers
at a river crossing

three stone-cold words
were all her parents had
to accompany them
to their graves

bayoneted on site

many a time I wonder
how she felt
when led to slaughter
on the bank of the
anonymous
crimson-tinged river

the dead exist
in the memories of the living
one day will it be as if
she had never lived at all?

September 2004

I was five years old. Though the war was everywhere around me, I had not been aware of it until then. What befell Yu Zhonghe literally brought it home to me—my first lesson of war. I had never heard of a *bayonet*, but I knew

Yu Zhonghe and admired her. To think someone so gentle and beautiful was bayoneted to death and thrown into the river… What kind of people would do that?

She died; we lived on. But I've never forgotten her or the beastly brutality of the Japanese. Though not privy to her family's grief, I could sense the house we shared was never the same. And one fateful night less than a year later, we had to run for our own lives from the Japanese. We never saw the Yu family again.

FOUR

My Years as Chang Tsen

1941-45

Iwas in first grade, basking in the glory of being *jizhang*, head of the class. I took great pride in my job. Each class period, at the beginning when the teacher entered and the end just before she left the classroom, I would call out lustily: "STAND UP," "BOW." The whole class would do accordingly. One night I went to bed as usual. When I woke up, everything in my world was gone—school, Mother, brother, sister, home...

"It was winter," my brother recalled recently. He was nine when it happened. "I woke up in the middle of the night because of someone pounding on the door. A woman rushed in. The next thing I knew I was standing on the bed, and Jiaojie, our maid, was buttoning my cotton quilt gown in a hurry."

On December 7, 1941, the Japanese not only attacked Pearl Harbor, but also sank all the American and British gunboats on the Huangpu River. Japanese troops simultaneously occupied the French Concession and the International Settlement (the British and American concessions) in Shanghai. All foreign nationals were arrested and placed in concentration camps—their sovereignty and extraterritorial privileges no more. For the Chinese, living in the French Concession or International Settlement no longer afforded any protection.

It was around the same time that the Japanese discovered who was working for the Resistance—and the addresses of their families. Because my mother had a job and didn't receive my father's salary, our names were at the bottom of the list, giving the others time to warn us. My mother was in bed nursing a broken ankle—she had fallen down on the stairs just days before. Somehow she managed to pack and get us out before the Japanese military police arrived.

I have always had a good memory. But try as I might, I don't remember a thing about that fateful night or the next six months, a time when my family was torn apart, with only my brother's patchy memory filling in the gaping hole. For me, the whole period was a blank—and still is, 70 years later. In my 50s, I went to psychiatrists, psychologists, therapists, hypnotists—you name it—to retrieve that part of my memory. Bodywork and deep-muscle massage are supposedly capable of bringing back old issues and long-lost memories. I tried those, too, all to no avail.

I must have been roused from sleep, dressed, and taken… *where*? Who were those strangers that kept me? Suddenly everybody in my family was gone. Would I ever see them again? Were they dead?

What were the real or imagined dangers in my six-year-old mind? What *happened* to make it shut off that portion of my life so decisively, never to surface again?

My brother remembers staying with the in-laws of my father's good friend Mei Guangyu, who always referred to him as his future son-in-law. Charley knew why he had to be there. He kept a low profile and played with the kids, including the girl who was supposedly his future bride. He never stepped out of the apartment, and never complained about not going to school.

But who were the strangers that kept me, for more than six months? Was it a family? Were they paid for it? How did my mother find them in the middle of the night and entrust me to them? Did she take me to one of the underground safe houses of the Resistance? Why did my mother never mention it later? In fact, my brother remembered that I did not stay at the same place the whole time. So I was passed along from one place to another? I don't recall a single friendly face or gesture.

I must not have gone to school either. How did I pass the time? Was it like solitary confinement? Chinese New Year must have come and gone. So did my seventh birthday. Everything is like an overexposed negative—irretrievably lost.

My mother did come to see me once and took me to a park. That is the only thing I remember from that six-month period. I was on a swing at a playground, and Mother was standing to my left. She brought me two new dresses, one a red and navy tartan.

I remember my homecoming. It must have been in May 1942, for there was still a chill in the air. Only years later did my brother and I deduce that our mother and sister must have stayed with our aunt and uncle, Yiniang and Shushu, during those months because after we arrived in our new home that day our sister arrived, a toddler still in her white rabbit fur winter coat. When she walked through the door,

she called our cousins' names, "Where's Xiaowei? Xiaodi?"
We must have looked like total strangers to her. In her
confusion and excitement, she slipped and fell.

Our father was sitting in the living room of our new
home, almost a stranger. I hadn't seen him for three years—
half of my lifetime. Mother had bought me a new, bright red
dress.

For the Chinese, red symbolizes good luck and happiness. It was *the* celebratory color to wear on happy occasions.
But I was not happy, and I was never fond of the color either.
That day that orange-red hue looked especially offensive.
From my perspective, I had been plucked from my warm,
cozy bed one night and thrust in with a pack of strangers for
what seemed a lifetime. Now, for reasons unknown to me,
my mother had brought me back to what seemed a joyous
family union and wanted me to wear red—*red*—the color of
a monkey's behind! Was she planning to throw me back to
those strangers again? I felt helpless, utterly alone, betrayed,
frightened.

"I hate red!" I blurted out.

Quick as a flash, my father slapped me hard on both
cheeks:

"Your mother bought you a new dress, and how dare you
say you don't like it!"

My mind turned off for an instant. All I could see was his
face, green and twisted with anger. In confusion and horror I
thought: *He hates me. My own father absolutely despises me! I knew
it! I knew it!* He never hit any of us before or after—this was
the only time.

I had no idea that my father, brought up in luxury and
idleness, with his good looks and charisma knowing nothing but success and pleasure, had been fighting in a hotly

contested area—the Shandong and Jiangsu War Zone, part of the Third War Zone, used to be under Chiang Kai-shek. The previous three years had been the most deadly and terrifying experiences in his life.

The Nationalists and Communists had agreed the year before to unite against the Japanese. Yet in practice, the Communists never abandoned their goal of overthrowing the Nationalist regime, "the tool of foreign imperialism in China." Often when the Nationalist forces, led by Han Deqin, the commander of the War Zone and my father's immediate superior, fought the Japanese in the south, the New Fourth Army of the Chinese Communists would attack Han from the north. (In addition to attacking the Nationalist forces from the rear, the Communists also used various deceptive tactics to win over the peasants in the countryside. My father's wartime experiences taught him never to trust the Communists.)

From 1939 until 1945 when we left Shanghai in the waning months of the war, my father came home only twice. This was his first time. He didn't show up for frivolous reasons like a family reunion. Sneaking back to Shanghai and out again was exceedingly dangerous, for it entailed passing through many Japanese checkpoints and patrol lines. Each time he made the trip, it was because the Resistance had suffered a serious blow, dealt not by the Japanese but by the Communists. He had literally no other place to go.

Once after a major military skirmish, Han escaped to the north while my father and a colleague became separated from Han and his troops, and went south. They managed to get a small boat and were on the river when the Japanese shot at them in the dark. The two bailed water all night to save the boat from sinking and managed to reach a village in the morning, only to be arrested by the Japanese. They didn't look at all like the locals, but armed with well-prepared stories—including fake names and telephone numbers—they were released after questioning.

Another time he was arrested with several other men and lined up for execution. The Japanese soldier killed one at a time, by plunging his bayonet into each man's gut with a twist. When it came to my father, the soldier spied his expensive watch, grabbed it, burst out laughing, and let him go.

After experiences like these, it was understandable that he would view my objection to the color of the new dress as extremely and inexcusably self-indulgent. More importantly, because of his law background, he was the director of the bureau of military law of the War Zone. In short, he was the court martial: he judged me guilty, and the sentence he carried out was swift and sure. Muscles have a long memory. Whenever I recall that moment, I can still feel my cheeks burn.

He was also a heavy snorer. In the few days while he was home, his snore, like a lion's roar, reverberated throughout the apartment. It kept me awake most of the night. One morning I woke up to discover that he had left. I didn't miss him.

Our new home was also in the French Concession, a second-floor apartment in a three-story house owned by an old White Russian couple at 275-C Rue de Pétain—named after the French marshal who, ironically, at that time was heading the Vichy government that was collaborating with Hitler.

My mother had managed to acquire forged identification papers for all of us, with false names. She became Mrs. Chang, maiden name Chao, given name Keling; my brother, Chang Ping, was supposed to be a nephew of her husband, a businessman; my sister became Chang Lining. I became Chang Tsen, the given name meaning "true" in Chinese, although my name was anything but true.

My forged identification card with my assumed name, Chang Tsen.

The card is in Chinese on one side, French on the other.

So the Chang family carried on with their lives. In the fall I enrolled in the second grade at Pétain Elementary School. My brother and I were warned never to divulge our real names, but our new maid knew. Mother had hired her before she retrieved us. Zhongying was from my father's hometown of Yangzhou. A young woman who had left home to seek employment in Shanghai to escape domestic abuse, she turned out to be extremely capable and loyal. She figured out early on that we were living under fake names, and why. Nevertheless, she stayed with us through thick and thin, until we left for Taiwan. My mother missed her, always holding her up as the gold standard of an excellent maid.

Our life on the Rue de Pétain was comfortable. We had white lace curtains in the windows and did not eat cornmeal pancakes. Under Mother's tutelage, Zhongying became an excellent cook.

The only dish she was squeamish about was stir-fried eel. The variety of eel sold at the market was like a medium-sized snake, with a diameter about the size of a quarter. Very much alive, the eel was kept in a bucket of water till dinnertime. Zhongying would chop it crosswise into pieces one and half inch in length and stir-fry it with fresh garlic, ginger, and scallions. It was tender, delicious beyond comparison, and relatively easy to make. But the eel was so full of life that its chopped pieces twitched on the board, as if they were in pain or trying to get away.

Life seemed to be on a normal course again, except that my childhood had been split in two. Someone sickly, a thin, quiet, and melancholy girl, replaced the healthy, chubby, happy-go-lucky six-year-old. I became a voracious reader, eagerly consuming anything with words on it. (Did I get anything to read in those months?)

During second grade I was walking to school one morning, when a group of boys began following me, chanting, "Four-eye frog! Four-eye frog!" I had started wearing glasses.

One day after school, my brother and I had gotten a bit rowdy, incurring the ire of our White Russian landlord downstairs. When our mother learned about it in the evening, she pushed us out the door of the apartment, declaring that she didn't want us anymore. It was dark outside; my brother and I huddled on the stairs, feeling abandoned and forlorn. True to his role as the older brother, he told me not to worry. He knew how to get to our aunt Yiniang's house; we would go there in the morning, and she would take care of us. After what seemed like half the night, the door opened. Mother took us back.

In Shanghai—perhaps only in the foreign concessions— English classes started in third grade. I was chosen to do "Twinkle, Twinkle, Little Star" in a poetry-reciting contest and had to stay after school to practice the words as well as hand gestures. I received first prize.

One month into fourth grade, when we were required to begin studying Japanese instead of English, I came down with a sore throat, and was too sick to go to school.

The timing was unfortunate. My father had just come home for the second time. Like the first time, he showed up at night with nothing except the rumpled dirty clothes on his back. No eyeglasses, fountain pen, or watch. My mother had to go out and buy him everything and equip him again for the road. We knew his stay would be brief. With frequent house searches and the Japanese police headquarters across the street, everyone in the family was tense, not celebratory. A few days went by, and nobody paid much attention to my sore throat.

One day my mother came back from work and asked how I was. My father said I was fine—quiet, no complaints. But she took it as a bad sign. Upon examination, she realized I had diphtheria ("white throat," as it is called in Chinese), a life-threatening, highly contagious disease. A serious discussion ensued. Taking me to the hospital could endanger the whole family, especially with my father in the house.

My next memory was in the emergency room of the hospital. I lay in bed, Wu Niangniang, my fifth aunt, Father's older sister, sat in a chair on my left. The doctor bent over me on my right. Right, left, right, left, right... He kept poking me with a syringe—inflicting great pain—in the crook of the elbow of alternate arms, looking for a usable vein, the whole time muttering, "Why did you bring her in so late? Another half hour and she could be dead." He explained to my aunt he was trying to give me *gamma globulin*, some kind of miracle drug I had never heard of before, a name I haven't forgotten since.

My mother's diagnosis was correct. It was diphtheria.

Wu Niangniang was chosen probably because she lived closest to us, although she didn't know it. Since we had moved to our new apartment, we had not divulged our address to any friends or relatives, so if questioned they could honestly say they didn't know where we lived. For safety reasons, my mother probably brought me to my aunt's apartment and asked her to take me to the hospital.

It was a children's hospital. I was admitted and stayed for weeks. Wu Niangniang must have left after getting me settled. She never came back. Again I found myself in a completely strange environment with no family around, except this time I was older and understood what was happening. I was sick. I was so sick from high fever and other symptoms that I didn't care where I was or how many days passed. Even now I can recall that awful head-swelling feeling.

When I became more aware of my surroundings, I found myself in a fairly large room with a roommate, a six-year-old boy with typhoid fever. Here was an enviable little fellow. I was always alone. My mother would drop by for a couple of minutes every few days, without ever sitting down, perhaps due to time constraints and safety concerns. But that boy—mother, father, aunts, uncles, and cousins constantly surrounded him. Luckiest of all, he had a doting grandmother who never left his side. She slept on a cot by his bed and attended to his every need.

Our beds were perpendicular to each other, separated by the door. There were no curtains for privacy. I watched his family bustle around him; sometimes I heard him make demands, and the grandmother try to pacify him, to make him more comfortable, her voice tender, soothing. I got the feeling that she would have cut her own heart out if it would only make him well.

I understood from the doctor and nurses' instructions to the family that the child was forbidden to eat—something about what it would do to his intestines. That point was made to the family repeatedly. But the boy was suffering from hunger and boredom. Who wouldn't be? One afternoon the grandmother broke down and fed him a half bowl of mung-bean porridge.

From the Chinese perspective, it was the least harmful food. According to Chinese traditional medicine, mung beans are good for ridding the body of toxins and reducing inflammation. She probably never believed in Western medicine in the first place. Unfortunately, typhoid fever was a Western disease.

That evening I was jolted awake by loud shrieks and cries. The boy had died, a few feet from where I slept. He was still and unmoved by the commotion around him, and he seemed to have shrunk a bit.

So this was death? My doctor had said *I* could have died, but dying was such an exotic concept that I didn't take him seriously. Now suddenly it was real. So I could be just like him, not knowing his family was crying around him. In my case, if I had died, my family wouldn't even know.

I turned my face to the wall. I couldn't bear to see the grandmother's grief, didn't dare to watch his body covered by white sheet, carried to the morgue. I tried to cover my ears to block out his mother's sobs when she packed up his belongings.

Finally all became quiet. Someone had switched off the light. I turned. His bed was empty. The room seemed to have grown. A stiff wind blowing outside threw moving shadows into the empty and menacing room.

All the ghost stories I had heard before came to mind. I was afraid to see ghosts, and more afraid to close my eyes. With my heart beating like a runaway freight train, I wondered how a boy who was moaning and complaining in the afternoon could be dead and gone by evening. Would I be cold like him, unconscious like him, lying in the morgue with other dead bodies like him? Shut in a dark and suffocating box like him? Would he become what we called a *stiff corpse* and come back to haunt me? My mind was like a hyperactive windmill, busily turning round and round.

I started having trouble falling asleep at night, and when I did sleep nightmares were persistent visitors. I've long since been able to marvel at how childish I was then, not knowing that living sometimes can be worse than dying, and that some people are far more frightening than ghosts.

Finally, my mother showed up one morning to take me home. She also brought me two small cans of food: braised bamboo shoots and braised gluten pieces. They tasted absolutely delicious in comparison to hospital food. To this day I simply can't resist them. I guess food is often more than what it is; sometimes the sustenance we get from it can be largely emotional. Those cans of food were the only sweet moment of my hospital trauma. I clutched them as a freezing person would clutch a warm blanket.

My excitement at returning home, however, was tempered by the realization that I had to be isolated in a room by myself. Diphtheria was highly contagious. Understandably, with my five-year-old sister around, my mother couldn't take a chance.

My mother got me settled and went to work. While Zhongying was busy in the kitchen, my sister lingered outside my door. I came up with a brilliant idea—I wrapped my face with a handkerchief and invited her in. I can still see her face today, timid yet curious, as she took tentative steps toward me. We had a nice time, though my handkerchief required constant adjustment. When my mother found out that evening, she was furious. I hadn't realized the air in my room was contagious.

Back to solitary confinement.

They say trouble always comes in twos. I was soon found to suffer from complications of diphtheria—inflammation of the lymph glands in the heart and lungs. The doctor ordered bed rest. I never went back to Pétain Elementary

School. The damage to my heart and lungs continued to crop up throughout my life. I had to be kept at home for a whole school year in junior high in Hangzhou, and for a semester in high school in Taiwan. I became the weakling of the family, first to get sick, last to get well.

One day my mother brought home two spools of yarn. She wanted to teach me to knit, but asked Zhongying to wash the yarn first. It turned out a street beggar had grabbed her paper sack and quickly spit on it, assuming it was bread. When he found yarn, he threw the bag on the pavement in disgust.

I didn't get very far with knitting; instead, I renewed my love affair with books. There was no library nearby and we had no books at home. But at almost every street corner in Shanghai, shabby shops rented books for a pittance. As long as one's legs didn't give out, one could stand there and browse or read. Before I got sick, my brother and I had spent many of our after-school hours and our small allowances there. Rarely were we able to splurge to buy an ice cream cone or a small French baguette.

Now that I was bedridden, I became the beneficiary of his largesse—whatever books struck his fancy and his allowance permitted him to rent. He loved serialized kung-fu novels. Occasionally translations of foreign works would be available at the shop, and even the four great Chinese classics: "Romance of the Three Kingdoms," "The Water Margin," "Journey to the West," and "Dream of the Red Chamber." A lot I didn't understand. But beggars couldn't be choosers, and I certainly was not picky, happily devouring whatever came to my hands.

While I was immersed in the world of books—soiled, yellowed, edges frayed and corners curled—I never dreamed that the first day I was allowed to be out of bed would be the day we left Shanghai forever.

It was February 1945, just past my 10th birthday. We didn't know it, but World War Two was entering its final stage. Residents of Shanghai were under orders to hang thick, black curtains on windows at night because of increasingly frequent American bombing raids. Our father arranged for us to leave Shanghai with a group of soldiers and low-ranking officers of the Resistance to flee to the interior of China. My immediate problem was learning how to walk, for my legs were weak and shaky from months of disuse. But my spirits were high. Like a bird released from its cage, I was elated to be out of bed. At first I walked with Zhongying's support, then without.

Leaving our apartment in the morning, the five of us, including Zhongying, traveled to Pudong, a neighboring county. There, we met up with the soldiers and officers, including the former Nationalist magistrate of Pudong. They were there to assist and protect us during the trip. Waiting until late at night, we set off for the beach. The men walked. We rode on the "moon cart"—what the Chinese poetically named *yi lun mingyue*, "a wheel of luminous moon."

It was a vehicle between the fabled sedan chair and the famous rickshaw—a large wheel with a handle in center back, steered by a coolie. A wooden board slightly larger than a bicycle seat on either side of the wheel could seat an adult or a child if weight was carefully balanced. These days if you are lucky, you might find one in a museum.

Once we reached the ocean's edge, the men carried us on their shoulders. They trudged in ankle- then knee- then thigh-high water to a small fishing boat with a top. In silence and darkness we were packed lying down at the bottom of the boat like sardines. All we could hear was the water—and shots. We were going through the Japanese patrol line. My brother became seasick. Someone passed him dried ginger pieces to chew to stave off nausea.

In the morning we arrived at Huangguoshu, south of Zhejiang province, still in Japanese-occupied territory. For a while we were carried in two-bearer sedan chairs, again a novelty for us. (For transportation in Shanghai we would hire a rickshaw or *sanlun che,* a three-wheeled vehicle, with a two-wheeled carriage pulled by a man pedaling an attached unicycle.) The sunny mountainside was covered with blooming azaleas. It *seemed* to be a perfect day for a pleasant outing.

But the constant danger of running into Japanese soldiers, the bombed-out highways and bridges, everything reminded us of war. Luckily, the Japanese forces were already in retreat; they largely left the rural areas alone. We never encountered any. But our group was such an obvious and suspicious target that we had to stick to the countryside, avoiding cities and public transportation, and staying with farmers or at lodgings. For quick getaways, we always slept with our clothes on.

From dawn to dusk, day after day, I've never seen so much countryside, so many tombs rising like giant pimples from the fields everywhere (there were no cemeteries in the rural areas), so many little sheds for worshipping small deities (they obviously weren't doing a very good job), and so many dark, filthy, smelly lodgings. Some offered bed and breakfast, others bed but no breakfast, still others neither. We spent many nights sleeping on cold, damp, and dirty floors.

Our family would crowd into one room, while the men sought shelter with nearby farmers. Meals were chancy. Two things stood out during the trip: hard-boiled eggs—whenever available—and walking, whenever sedan chairs were unavailable or impractical. At times my sister was carried on one of the men's shoulders. The rest of us trudged or dragged ourselves along, from south of Zhejiang, westward to north of Fujian province, to northeast of Jiangxi province—for about four months. Finally we left Japanese-occupied territory and reached Wudu village in Yanshan county, Jiangxi province, where we waited for our father.

I remember during the journey how I, naturally squeamish and timid, dreaded stepping on rocks or wading across small streams. There were many. But they were nothing compared to crossing mountains. The winding mountain paths, at times slippery with rain and mud, was so narrow that we had to walk in single file. On one side rising straight up was the slick, solid mountain; the other side dropped straight down thousands of feet, to water running rapidly over jagged rocks. My legs would desert me, and I had a strong urge to sit down, never to get up again. But Mother wouldn't let me; her calm voice kept urging, "Don't look down there. Just watch your feet and put one foot in front of the other."

Putting one foot in front of the other, I bid farewell to my years as Chang Tsen.

FIVE

Those Invisible Wounds of War

Once over, those years spent escaping from the Japanese military police, living in hiding under assumed names, and the long, perilous journey—such an important, formative period of our lives—became a taboo topic in our family. Never a word from our father, not even an allusion, as if those six years had never happened. Consequently, my mother and the three of us never spoke of it, either. As time passed, my memories about those years faded; they seemed to dissipate, like a nightmare that had never existed.

When my father became garrulous in his old age, he once did mention that period, about the first time he left home to join the Resistance in 1939—how he refused to hold my baby sister and headed straight for the door. As usual, his words stopped at just the place for me to murmur my agreement or admiration. Period. No questions or discussion. While his patriotism was laudable, what he said nonetheless triggered a pain buried in my heart, a pain I couldn't put into words at the time...

It was deep resentment and anger, for his callous disregard and lack of recognition for what we—especially my mother—had to suffer. It was not what he did, but what he didn't do.

I was too young to know what my mother's life was like after he took off in 1939, leaving her with three small children, the baby not yet one-year old; leaving us with no means of support and my mother with constant worry about his safety. I was never told how she made the transition from her real name to a fake one, holding the same job. But I do know more about her life when we lived under assumed names on the Rue de Pétain.

From 1942 to 1945, for three years, more than 1,000 days, with her fake identification card in her purse, she shuttled among various doctors' offices. She never said a word to us about the humiliation she must have felt running into former classmates practicing medicine, while she, the top student in her class, peddled medicine.

But the humiliation must have paled in comparison to the danger of the situation—that her old acquaintances might recognize her or inadvertently divulge her true identity. In transit between doctors' offices, she constantly braved Japanese checkpoints. Many times a day, machine-gun-toting, bayonet-bearing Japanese soldiers would blow a whistle, close off a street, and check identifications. Each time she had to steel herself, attempting to stay calm so she could get through safely.

Every morning she went to work, not knowing whether she would make it home that night. If she got caught, it would be the end of all of us. None of our relatives and friends knew our new address or assumed names. If anything had happened to my mother, they would not have been able to find us.

Returning home at night didn't guarantee safety, either. Oftentimes in the dead of night, we would be jerked awake by the sounds of soldiers marching outside, and quiver under our sheets while their heavy boots approached our house. Finally came the loud pounding on the door. By then we would all be up and waiting in the living room. Mother would order Zhongying, terrified and trembling, to open the door. They would barge in, bayonets clinking, while Mother sat serenely, identification cards and answers ready. Sometimes they would make a point of searching every room; at other times they didn't bother. I made a point of not looking at their faces or listening to the orders they barked.

On occasions like these, we were *mum as chilled cicadas*, to use a Chinese expression. These experiences planted in my mind a profound bitterness toward Japan that manifested itself in unexpected ways throughout my life.

In 1971, our family of four was to spend a year in Denmark where my husband Sam was to be a visiting professor at the University of Copenhagen. My parents persuaded us to use the opportunity to visit them in Taiwan by purchasing around-the-world tickets. Our first stop was Tokyo. It was shocking to find Tokyo a bustling, prosperous, world-class metropolis a quarter century after the Japanese surrender. People everywhere looked proud and happy, enjoying their good lives. Our long-suppressed, bitter memories of the war surged. Sam, two years my elder, had lived in Chongqing—the war capital—during the war, and recalled seeing, after the Japanese bombings, the junction of the Yangtze and Jialin rivers strewn with corpses, staining the waters red. As a child, running for his life with his family to the bomb shelter, with the Japanese planes screaming overhead, he had to step over bodies and ignore the wounded, moaning and pleading for help. We left Tokyo after one day instead of three days as planned. Neither of us set foot in Japan again, except for plane stops.

When we wanted to buy a piano for our daughter when she was nine, I discovered I simply could not choose a Japanese one—the emblazoned Japanese name was too offensive. Instead, I searched high and low for a different make and found an obscure American brand named "Krakauer," a decent upright, now in my son Clif's home.

To this day, I still resist purchasing Japanese products. It would be unthinkable for me to buy Japanese cars, televisions, household appliances, computers, or other electronics. Even for small items I have been known to go out of my way to look for non-Japanese brands. It does make life more difficult, given the preponderance of Japanese products in this country, but I simply can't help it.

My scars from the war lead to unusually strong reactions when I watch war films, especially those involving the Imperial Japanese army. Having been rendered supersensitive about bayonets, I was emotionally shaken for days when I chanced upon photos of babies carved right out of their mothers' abdomens, babies tossed in the air, while the perpetrating Japanese soldiers laughing uproariously… I even felt threatened in a surprisingly deep and visceral way by the energy in the room when a group of seniors punched the air in an exercise class.

It would be easier to forgive and forget if Japanese behavior after the war was less heinous. Sadly, Japan *is* the country that devastated China, but has not paid a single penny of war reparations. It *is* the country that, unlike Germany, didn't apologize for or even admit its atrocities. It *is* the country that went so far as to revise its textbooks to read that its army *entered* China, not invaded China. It *is* the country that funded movies and an opera—that I saw—which twisted historical facts to show Japan in a favorable light. It *is* the country with people and organizations that hounded the brilliant young historian, Iris Chang, with death threats after her book "The Rape of Nanking: The Forgotten Holocaust of World War II" was published. Depressed, she took her own life at 36, leaving a husband of 13 years and a son aged two.

For six long years, my mother was tormented by worries about my father's safety. She saw him twice, each time for a few days. At the same time, she raised three small children single-handedly, met the social demands of her in-laws and other relatives and friends, and held down a job to support all of us.

Although she managed everything exceptionally well, she was not made of steel. Those years of relentless, tremendous pressure took their toll. Her shiny black hair turned dry and thin. She began to suffer from many health problems, including beriberi, ulcers, and heart disease. Doctors prescribed tranquilizers and smoking. After the war she came down with inflammation of the inner membrane of the heart and was bedridden for months.

One year my son Clif, working in Silicon Valley, turned 34. I called to wish him a happy birthday. The moment I put down the phone, it occurred to me that he was now the same age as my mother when she limped with a broken ankle to flee the Japanese military police with three little ones in tow. And when my mother took us on that grueling, perilous four-month journey from Shanghai to reunite with our father, she was only as old as my daughter Andrea that year, 37.

The Chinese poet Beidao declared, "This is an era with no heroes." He was referring to the era of the Cultural

Revolution. I believe every era has its heroes, they just aren't always known. Not once, not twice, but daily for six long years my mother performed heroically. One false move, a little tremor, or a tiny wrong gesture, could have given her away and wiped out all of us. She was indeed a hero. *My* hero.

But heroes are human too, and being human, they are vulnerable. They may be calm and brave at times of crisis. But afterward, won't they need their loved ones, those they sacrificed for, to express a bit of appreciation?

My mother was unhappy during the latter part of her life. She told me that Father, without informing her, gave away her apartment on the Rue de Pétain, and sold for next to nothing the cartons of expensive medicine that she had hoarded for sale after the war. She was never a miser, but she was bitter about that. Could it have something to do with not being acknowledged or treated with respect or consideration?

I listened to her, but remained silent, a deplorable lifetime habit. Sensing her intense pain, my overwhelming desire was to provide a shoulder for her to cry on, so to speak. I wanted her to be able to talk and relieve some of her long-held pain. Now I bitterly regret not offering her succor by asking questions. Questions about those years would have given her a chance for once to speak her piece; questions, the answers to which *I desperately needed*. However, inhibited by the taboo, I missed my once-in-a-lifetime opportunity.

The only time I ever ventured to ask her why I was the only one entrusted to the strangers, she answered: "Because you were the most obedient."

And how I wished my father wouldn't always dismiss her with "what do *you* know?" How I longed for him to say for once *during those years, if it hadn't been for your mother…* Ten simple, little words. They wouldn't have cost anything, but they might have served to heal, to bind her wounds, and in the process, might have helped to heal the rest of us, too.

Those ten words could have been the key to break open the taboo, to start all of us reminiscing, and to unite us as a family, to overcome the perennial separation, the cold top-to-bottom, Father-knows-everything-we-know-nothing hierarchy we were obligated to uphold.

My paternal grandfather died at 42 when my elder uncle was away in France pursuing his Ph.D. studies. My father became the head of the family at the tender age of 10. Could that have contributed to his being a man who found it impossible to put himself in others' shoes or, to see other people's points of view?

In the years of my parents' happy beginnings, as symbolized by their engagement photo, they were confident they were at the forefront of change. In fact, Chinese society was teetering on

My paternal grandfather

the cusp of change. But unfortunately, they themselves were the descendents of *five thousand years of history and culture*, as Chinese are wont to proclaim. They had a thoroughly modern wedding. It was easy to have a modern wedding, but extremely difficult—if not impossible—to have a modern marriage, and to think and behave in an entirely new, modern manner. It was so easy, perhaps inevitable, for them to slip into their traditional roles and traditional thinking…

My parents had no way of knowing that soon enough, they would be overtaken by the capriciousness and rapaciousness of life. Who can blame them? To be young is to be unaware. Unaware of one's own limitations, of life's travails—its perils and pitfalls—and of the most crushing adversary of all: war.

My father probably felt completely justified in letting my mother do the heavy lifting, as far as family was concerned. Wasn't that what a wife and mother was supposed to do? After all, those six years he spent in the Shandong and Jiangsu War Zone were the most dangerous and terrifying in his life. For someone accustomed to luxury and idleness, he deserved much credit for steadfastly braving the dangers. He was certainly no coward.

But was he threatened by my mother's surprising courage and capabilities, or simply ashamed of letting her be the sole breadwinner during the war? Judging from how he reneged on his promise to her and to his father-in-law to allow her to practice medicine, and how adamant he was in keeping her from work after the war, I sometimes wonder: could it have been simply his male ego?

After all, in Chinese patriarchal society, being male meant never having to say you were sorry. Or thank you.

I will never know.

SIX

The Interlude

1945-1947

Our arduous trip from Shanghai ended at Wudu, a tiny village with a grandiose name—five capitals. Although not a single capital could be found, we were delighted that there was a YMCA where we could stay to wait for our father's arrival. In no time at all our maid Zhongying started cooking. The first meal she made was braised pork with fresh fava beans and bamboo shoots. After four months of hard-boiled eggs and not much else, it was the most delicious food I had ever had. In my years in California, where fresh fava beans and bamboo shoots were available, I tried repeatedly to make the same dish, but never managed to replicate the taste, until I realized I lacked the most important ingredient of all—four months of food deprivation.

My brother and I were sent to the only school in the village: a single room with all grades. My brother a junior high student, and I, technically still a fourth grader, were lumped together with a handful other kids. We were told to go outside, where there was just a patch of concrete, with no playground or any equipment, not even a ball to throw around. With the sun beating down on us, it was hot—and boring. After a week of being scorched and learning nothing, we convinced our mother to let us quit.

Years later, when sun-dried tomatoes became all the rage in the States, I remembered what my brother and I called ourselves that week—sun-dried people. Having been outdoors from dawn to dusk daily for four months, we were certainly no strangers to the sun—or other elements for that matter—but the sun in Wudu seemed more powerful than in all the other places we had been except Guizhou.

Our father arrived soon after. He had helped wrap up the Resistance operation in northern Jiangsu province before heading to Shanghai. From there he took the faster, easier, but more dangerous river route, and was therefore able to arrive almost at the same time, even though he had started out much later.

He was not alone. With him was our cousin Paul, Wu Niangniang's oldest son, a lad of 17 with a shy smile and goofy nature. The last time we had seen him was before the war when we stayed in Yangzhou at the ancestral home, when I was about a year old. My mother remembered him as a pampered boy. At nine years old, he still had a personal nurse-maid following him closely wherever he went, pleading at his every step, "Little Master, do be careful; lest you fall." Shortly after we left Yangzhou, however, his father died. The war drove his mother from her home in Yangzhou to Shanghai, where she remarried. Because their quarters in Shanghai were rather cramped, Paul was put in a Catholic orphanage. He played the saxophone in the orphanage band that performed at funerals to make a little money for the institution. When my father went to see his older sister Wu Niangniang in Shanghai, she asked him to find an apprentice job for Paul, as he was getting too old for the orphanage and had no place to go. She was more than delighted when my father offered to take Paul with him and raise him as one of his own.

That was how Paul joined our family. Since he was older than we were, we were told to address him as *Zhongyi gege*, his Chinese name being Zhongyi—by coincidence very similar to our maid Zhongying's name. *Gege* means elder brother.

Paul regaled us with stories; two stood out in my mind. One night he was asleep when he felt someone open the mosquito net over his bed. He saw it was his father, who was supposedly more than a hundred miles away in Shanghai. Later, news reached them that his father had died that same night. (The Chinese believe that the dead come back to look in on the family and collect the footsteps left in life.)

When he first arrived at the orphanage, he felt too lazy to shower and decided to sit the time out. Suddenly water sprayed out of the showerhead. Startled, he jumped up and began to soap himself. Just when he had smeared soap all over, the water stopped. Shower time was over.

"What did you do?" we asked him.

"What else could I do? Put my clothes back on and pretended everything was fine."

We soon moved into quarters in the abandoned house of what must have been the wealthiest family in the village. We had to share the space with a young couple, the husband a platoon leader by the name of Zhang. They lived on one side, and we on the other; in the middle was the family ancestral temple.

Mrs. Zhang dreamed one night that a man approached her to say he was one of the ancestors in the family temple, and he intended to marry her. He told her his name. In the morning she found that very name among the long rectangular ancestral plates reposing on the altar of the temple. Indignant and frightened, she threw the plate in the outhouse, an act that enraged the ghost, who started to haunt her with threats of revenge in her dreams. She became desperately ill. Doctors, monks, exorcists—no one could help her. Finally she was put on a door and carried away from the house. On route, she suddenly jumped up yelling, "He's after me again!" and died.

My father's boss, Governor Han, lived nearby. We called him Han Bobo, (Elder Paternal Uncle Han). Han Bobo had lost his wife in childbirth during the war. The breeched baby, a son, did not survive, but they had a daughter a year younger than I. Now that the war was nearly over, he was considering remarriage. Someone arranged to have a soprano from the Shanghai School of Music travel all the way to Jiangxi as a candidate. Her stay with us provided my first exposure to Chinese classical vocal music.

By that I don't mean Chinese opera, which is a different genre altogether, something I knew practically nothing about at that time either. In Shanghai we heard only pop songs, many of which I still know by heart. But this not very young lady, probably 30, was singing songs with lyrics from poems, including one from the classic novel "Dream of the Red Chamber" that I had read in Shanghai. I was fascinated by the music as well as the lyrics, which I learned by heart from listening to her. I still remember those songs. She was not a very good soprano, and she liked to put on airs. We had fun watching Paul mimick her practicing her scales behind her back. Han Bobo didn't seem to think much of her either, as she soon disappeared from the scene.

Sadly, the only reading material my brother and I had in those months left with her—her volumes of the Chinese translation of the biography of the French writer Romain Rolland.

Our house was crowded and chaotic with men from the Resistance talking and arguing about what to do after the war. Mother was preoccupied with the logistics of running the inflated household. Zhongying, with the help of a private soldier we called Xiao Wei, served meals to a crowd whose number varied from meal to meal. We didn't know it then, but this was to be the pattern whenever our father was in residence.

One day the dinner was especially delicious. Everybody marveled about how tasty it was. Soon after, though, everyone came down with diarrhea. It happened that Xiao Wei always carried two large bottles to the market every day. One contained tea oil for cooking, the other tung oil for the lamps at night. That morning the two bottles got switched by mistake, and Zhongying used tung oil for cooking instead.

When the long-awaited victory came on August 15, 1945, it was almost an anticlimax for our family and guests. I don't remember celebratory firecrackers. Everyone in Wudu had only one thing in mind—going home.

It had taken us four months to travel through Japanese-occupied territory from Shanghai to Wudu, but the trip back, with long-distance buses and boats, took only about two weeks. But we didn't go back to Shanghai; we settled down in Hangzhou, the city with the famous, beautiful West Lake. I think my mother would have preferred to return to Shanghai and work her way back to medicine. But it was not up to her. Our father had given away the apartment on the Rue de Pétain. More importantly, he didn't think she should work now that he was once more the head of the house.

We lived in the center of town, near a famous noodle shop, *Kui Yuan Guan—guan* means restaurant. The taste and variety of their noodles were simply out of this world, *the* best noodles or pasta I've ever had. The Hans also lived nearby; Han Bobo had married a school teacher from Sichuan. His daughter and cousins told us that the noodles of that restaurant were extraordinarily delectable because of the power of a family of fox fairies. Every single day they witnessed a group of fox fairies moving across the rooftops on their way to the noodle shop to be fed. Many Chinese believed in the supernatural powers of fox fairies, which look like ordinary foxes. If you were on their good side, they would do wonders for you. But they were also capable of mischief, including turning into beautiful maidens to bewitch unsuspecting, poor, young scholars. I had heard and read plenty of stories about them.

As I was writing this, I thought I'd look up the noodle shop online. Lo and behold—time, wars, the Cultural Revolution—nothing succeeded in destroying this place. It's still there and thriving, listed as a must-visit location in Hangzhou, complete with road directions, and photos and prices of its most popular noodle dishes.

You've got to hand it to the fox fairies.

The center of town had all the theaters. One showed American films, at the time many Esther Williams movies. There were no subtitles, but each member of the audience was handed a printed sheet with synopsis.

After the War We Discovered Movies

How we loved to sit
in that dank, unkempt theater
watching other lives unfold—
lives at times lurid or tragic, but always
exciting and glamorous. No more
dreaded curfews, air raid sirens,
crossing checkpoints with fake documents.
Eyes glued to the screen, we saw
ourselves up there, living
charmed lives of movies.

Often, a sudden screech and a groan
brought the projector to a halt.
Aroused from our trance
by rude lights, we'd watch
the projectionist, fingers flying,
as he patched the celluloid
in his upper balcony booth.
At last the characters return,
carry on with their lives
oblivious of the interruption.
And I, in my pre-pubescence,
blissfully unaware—
real lives once broken
can never be the same again.

March 2005
Final revision, July 2007

Soon we moved from downtown to the edge of the city, into a two-story European style house, and Mother set her sights on my attending seventh grade in Hungdao Girls' High School, a private missionary school, the best in the city. But a serious hurdle loomed—the entrance examination.

I could sense the importance of my passing this exam when my mother rode with me in our family rickshaw that morning. Along beautiful West Lake, the willow and peach trees were budding; the scent of spring was in the air. Everything seem to spell hope and a new beginning.

The first test, unfortunately, was math, with ten problems. Not having had any math since the first month of fourth grade, I knew nothing about decimals, fractions, or word problems about putting chickens and rabbits in the same cage or planting trees in a row. The only problem I attempted was one with all kinds of parentheses and brackets. I wasn't even sure I did that one right. When my mother found out what had happened, she was so upset that she immediately went home, abandoning me to face my failures alone.

Perhaps it spoke more about the quality of my fellow contestants' performances than mine, I passed—to my mother's surprise and mine. Thus started my two years at Hungdao, the reputed school for "the nobility."

The school got its reputation perhaps from the fact that President Chiang Kai-shek's granddaughter Chiang Xiaozhang was across the street attending Hungdao Elementary School. I seem to remember her older brother Chiang Xiaowen was there too. I probably saw him once or twice. Hungdao Elementary School took both boys and girls, but its high school was only for girls. Chiang Xiaozhang was likely in fifth grade, beautiful and bigger-boned than her classmates. At that time what we called *huenxue* children, Eurasians, or mixed blood, were exceptionally rare. Chiang Kai-shek's son, Chiang Chingkuo, had been sent to Russia in his youth and had married a Russian, and their daughter was strikingly attractive.

My sister, a third grader by then, attended the same elementary school. My brother and Paul were in a boys' missionary high school nearby. Every morning all four of us would set out for school together; Paul would ride his bike with me sitting behind, while my brother carried my sister on his.

Lunch, delivered from home, was a rather elaborate affair by today's standards, with three dishes and a soup kept hot in a Chinese lunch box in the shape of a cake carrier with several compartments, stacked one on top of the other. It was smaller than a cake carrier in circumference, more like a layered cylinder with a handle on top. In the winter it also came equipped with a cotton quilt cover, like a tea cozy. But delivering four hot lunches to separate schools soon proved too much even for our capable Zhongying, now a housekeeper with a cook working under her. Soon we were all eating lunches provided by our respective schools.

Unlike today's high school cafeterias, Hungdao's dining room served three meals a day, because the school offered room and board to senior high students, many still displaced by war. In spite of its reputation of being the school for the nobility, Hungdao's lunches—rice, two meat and two vegetarian dishes and a soup—were definitely designed with economy in mind. Belt fish and cabbage, being the cheapest, made the most frequent appearances. Vegetables boiled with a few shreds of fatty pork qualified as a meat dish. It was institutional food, but in winter a hot pot, with red, burning coals underneath and boiling water in the pot, would be available at each table. We would gleefully dump all the dishes and soup into the hot pot. Somehow heating them mixed together made the whole thing more palatable, leaving everyone warm and satisfied.

Some of our teachers were American missionaries, speaking Chinese with a peculiar accent and wearing bright-colored dresses despite being elderly. The pressure to convert to Christianity was intense. After all, the school's name was Hungdao, which in Chinese literally means spreading the gospel truth. But I was never tempted. From the way they depicted God, omniscient and omnipotent, I figured I already had one like him at home.

I was not a good student. I did fine in every subject except algebra, which I failed for two years in a row. Each time I failed, I had to take a make-up exam in the summer. I did always manage to squeeze by in the make-up exam to go on to the next year. I could blame my ineptitude in algebra on having skipped three previous grades, but the truth was that I didn't pay much attention to algebra in class because I was always drawing pictures. My seatmate loved to draw pretty girls in different clothes and poses. I tried to copy her, but I couldn't draw noses, except in profile. And the algebra book had an advantage—its pages had many empty spaces that I could block out to sketch my "prima donna" in profile. Later in high school in Taiwan I was sometimes asked by different classmates to sketch their profiles. Once in a while I would succeed in catching some facial characteristic or bringing out a bit of personality, but I never progressed beyond pencil drawings.

I still have one I did of my mother during her last years in Maryland. It was a spur of the moment idea to divert her, and the sketch was not a very good rendering. I was always especially clumsy around my mother; doing that sketch was no exception. My mother and I were not alike. I have never been capable like her. I didn't inherit her beauty. I was never interested in medicine and remained terrified at the mere sight of blood. But we were similar in small, unexpected ways. We were the exact same height when young. I've never had her beauty, or stoism, or elegance, but I do have her stubborn streak. In old age in the mirror, I occasionally spot an expression that was peculiarly hers. On that day, she sat docilely, waiting for me to finish—her life's struggles and bitter disappointments behind her. For a moment, she seemed at peace. I felt emotionally drawn to her, incredibly, unprecedentedly close to her.

There was another reason for my mediocre performance in my studies—my heart was not in them. We had no school library, and I didn't know whether there was a city library or how to get to it. But my fellow schoolmates seemed to have an inexhaustible supply of books I could borrow. I went crazy with the opportunity, borrowing anywhere from one to three books a day. Most of them had to be returned the next day, so I read them surreptitiously during classes— hiding them under textbooks—during

Pencil sketch that I made of my mother at rest.

recess and all my waking hours, when possible. I read them

while brushing my teeth, washing my face, combing my hair, walking to and from school, any chance I had.

Translations of foreign novels were readily available in those years. I remember being enthralled by "The Three Musketeers" by what the Chinese called "Big Dumas" and "The Lady of the Camellias" by the "Little Dumas." My extracurricular readings depended entirely on availability. Again, beggars couldn't be choosers. I read a lot of Chinese romance novels by the famous Chang Hengshui and the popular and much inferior Feng Yuqi who always described the complexion of a beautiful girl's face as "a newly peeled egg."

Somehow I scraped together enough money to buy two thick volumes of "Gone with the Wind" translated by Fu Donghua; it became my prized possession. Books were my sole escape to another world. In the summer I would read translations of Russian novels left at home by my father when he was away in Shanghai. There weren't many. Wading through those excruciating Russian names was hard work, but once in a while, some passage would break through age, language, cultural, and all other barriers and speak directly to me, the young, impressionable reader. Reading Ivan Turgenev's "Fathers and Sons," I understood nothing of its philosophical or political discussions, but when the young protagonist is dying from typhus, and his father gazes from the doorway at him with such pain—desperation, helplessness, and love—it was like a poignant scene in a movie imprinted forever in my mind. To this day, whenever I think of it, it still shakes me to my foundations.

My father was away in Shanghai a great deal, for weeks, sometimes months at a time. In later years my brother told me that our father went into business, buying and shipping salt from somewhere in the interior to be sold in Shanghai. He never bothered to say goodbye before he left and we never knew when he would be back. One time, unfortunately for me, he was home.

Our house was right by the old city wall, at 30 West Surrounding City Road. There were no neighbors. We four children not only went to school together, by necessity we also played together after school. We played hide and seek, *ti jianze* (a game by kicking a homemade device—a coin sewn in cloth with two chicken feathers on top—to the air and catching it with your foot), and another game whose name I don't remember. The two boys were older and not always nice about playing with us. My sister, being the youngest and my father's obvious favorite, enjoyed better treatment. Sometimes I felt I was being picked on.

At play one day, I thought they were especially mean to me and decided to seek revenge. In the morning I got up early and sneaked downstairs where the two boys were asleep and struck them with my hand on their foreheads, lightly, once each. I was venting my resentment, as if to say, "Hey, look, I don't like the way you guys treated me."

I went back to bed, feeling rather pleased with myself for having carried out my revenge successfully. The next thing I knew, my father barged into the room I shared with my sister and demanded to know what I had done.

Whenever our father was home these days, he was never alone. A crowd of admiring friends always surrounded him; they literally basked in his glory. The Chinese expression is *zhong xin gong yue,* a crowd of stars surrounding and worshiping the moon. Suave, handsome, charming, eloquent, with a great sense of humor, he always outshone everyone, forever the center of attention. Years later in this country when I first encountered the word "charisma," I grasped its meaning instantly—that which my father possessed. Other than the time in Shanghai when he slapped me, I had never seen him angry, which made his fury that much more terrifying.

In our household children had no right to speak, and I was not an articulate child. In front of my father, by far the most articulate person I knew, I was more tongue tied than ever, especially in the face of his extreme rage. I was numb with fear. My little act of revenge was stupid enough, but sensing his ire, I did something worse. I stammered that I had done nothing; my denial only exacerbated his wrath.

The way you are, you will never have happiness in your life. No man will want you when you grow up. If you get married, your marriage will fail.

Delivered one at a time, those words were like a curse. Although only 11 years old, I could sense something was not right—the punishment didn't fit the crime. But one thing was unmistakable: he hated me, and I didn't know why. Why was I such a pariah? How could I survive an episode like this? I did the only thing I could do: pretending it never happened, or it didn't affect me, I went on. I endured it, as one endures hostile forces of nature, for I had no choice.

There was no doubt in my mind that he was right. If he found me hateful, I must have been so; I just didn't know what to do about it, except to try to stay out of his way, which was not difficult.

I was too young to know that life never stays the same; it always changes. My life changed beginning with the arrival of Nainai, my paternal grandmother.

SEVEN

The Magnolia Was Blooming

1947-1949

My family had its first taste of victory when after fleeing Shanghai in the waning days of war, we reached the territory unoccupied, probably never occupied by the Japanese. It was such relief to not have to constantly look over our shoulders to check for danger, and to not have to submit to random house searches at night by the Japanese military police, that we didn't mind living in a remote village with no electricity or running water. Two months later when the two atomic bombs dropped by the Americans brought about the Japanese surrender on August 15, 1945, our whole nation was euphoric. Nobody knew the ecstasy would be short-lived.

What the Japanese envisioned as a mere three-month battle had lasted eight years, one month, and three days. Towards the end of the protracted war, many Chinese, including my family, dared to hope for and dream about *shenli huanxiang*, returning home after the victory. Four simple Chinese words packed with so much pathos and longing. When the victory finally came, it was a victory at great expense. The war had devastated the country and its ruling party, the Nationalist or Kuomintang Party—a patient sapped by a serious prolonged illness was called upon to struggle up from his sickbed to fight a new, stronger opponent.

While the Nationalists employed their best troops against the Japanese in the 22 major battles—involving more than 100,000 soldiers on both sides—of the war, the Communists only participated in two, preferring to "save and preserve our strength and wait for favorable timing." According to a 1940 secret report by Zhou Enlai, the number two Chinese Communist leader, to the Soviet leader Stalin, only 40,000, or four percent of the one million Chinese military casualties at that point in the war, were from the Communist armies.

The Japanese apparently regarded the Nationalists, not the Communists, as their major opponent. The wartime capital, Chongqing, where Chiang Kai-shek was based, suffered the heaviest bombing of any city in the world to date.

The Communists knew they profited greatly from the war. When the People's Republic of China and Japan established formal diplomatic relations in 1972, Mao Zedong met with the Japanese Prime Minister Kakuei Tanaka. To Tanaka's apology for invading China, Mao responded that no apology was needed, because Japan's invasion had made "a great contribution" to China. Without the war, in Mao's own words, the Communists would not have been able to defeat Chiang Kai-shek and overthrow the Nationalists.

As I mentioned in the previous chapter, the victory in 1945 did not return us to Shanghai. Instead, we settled in Hangzhou, a four-and-a-half-hour train ride from Shanghai. There we lived for three years, until the civil war caught up with us and we had to flee again, this time to the remote island of Taiwan.

Fast forward 55 years. I was in my daughter Andrea's home when her baby Sylvia took sick. Suspecting that her firstborn might be allergic to house dust, Andrea gathered up all of Sylvia's stuffed animals to put away temporarily. I was shocked to see half a roomful of them in every size and description. It hit me that I had never held, or even seen a stuffed animal in my childhood—or a doll, for that matter. When I later told an American-born friend, she asked in puzzlement and innocence, "Why didn't you make one?"

I had never thought of it. I didn't seem to have a need for them. I guess that war and its attendant issue of survival have an overwhelming power to concentrate one's mind.

I was two years old when the Battle of Shanghai raged mere blocks away from the French Concession where we lived. For the following eight full years, we knew nothing but war. Even before it reached us, before it had us firmly in its grip, our lives were already touched by it, for all of my parents' decisions were informed by it. Once it was over, we tried to live normal, peaceful, happy lives but were forever scarred by it.

Our three years in Hangzhou, 1946-49, the last stage of my childhood, were the only peaceful time I knew in the first fourteen years of my life. Perhaps it was not a coincidence that when I tried to write poetry in English in my old

age as part of my legacy to my children and grandchildren,
I chose to write the first poem about war—in memory of
Yu Zhonghe, the first person I knew who died at the hands
of the Japanese. My second poem was about my first experience with peace, with normal life, when everyone's concerns and behavior are different from those of wartime.
This poem, "The Magnolia Tree," was written in memory
of my paternal grandmother. As I try to write about that
period, to evoke its mood and tenor, to revisit it with a lin-
gering look, it seems to acquire a bittersweet, dreamlike,
storied quality of its own. I treasure the memory still.

The Magnolia Tree

Imprisoned in her upstairs room
by age and bound feet
Nainai* appeared happiest
when blooms came out
on the magnolia tree.

So eagerly she leaned out the window
to hook the branches
clutching her cane
by the tip.

So gingerly she entrusted the flowers
to our waiting palms
as if they were so many
exquisite jewels.
The petals, plump and fragrant
were dipped in batter
fried, and dusted with sugar.

With each bite we savored
she would beam.

She even smiled
on those rare afternoons.

Under father's pen
in his genealogy tome
she seemed a saint,
but she only comes alive
for me
when I recall
the magnolia tree.

—January 2005

*Chinese for paternal grandmother

Nainai

The magnolia tree bloomed early in the spring of 1948 when I had just turned 13. Its buds came out around the beginning of March, bursting to their full glory by the middle of the month, as if seized by some inner sense of urgency. Not long after, the climbing tea roses and peonies followed suit, transforming the desolate front yard into a colorful, fragrant garden.

Over the years, the magnolia tree grew tall and massive, its boughs reaching all the way to the second floor, its pale, pink blossoms swaying seductively in the breeze outside Nainai's bedroom window. As she watched the flowers, she seemed to come alive. And when she deemed it was time, she would stand by her open window and use the crook of her walking cane to hook some of the branches inside— flowers, leaves and all.

My younger sister Lining and I would join in the adventure, our job to take the gathered petals downstairs to the kitchen. Nainai knew the plump magnolia petals made a delicious snack when dipped in a batter of eggs, flour, and sugar and fried in hot oil. She was right. Sweet and soft in the center and crispy on the outside, the fried petals had a way of filling our palate with their delicate fragrance while satisfying our need for something of substance.

As everyone enjoyed the snack, Nainai would look happy and proud. She acted as if she'd grown the flowers herself, as well as fried them. Only during these times would a slight smile appear on her face, making her look almost kind, even approachable. It was a pity that she would retreat into herself the rest of the time.

Nainai had a disproportionately large head and a rectangular face, the shape of a mahjongg tile. Her eyebrows sat high above her eyes; the eyelids were so deep set that, seen from afar, they looked like an additional set of eyebrows. The corners of her mouth were turned perpetually downward in a sullen, aggrieved manner. Most elderly women tended to be somewhat garrulous, but Nainai was an exception. She seldom opened her mouth, certainly never tried to speak to my sister or me or smile at us, never asked how we were, or patted our hands like those sweet, dimpled grandmothers of the storybooks.

When Nainai was brought the year before from my elder uncle's home to live in our house, she was unable to climb the stairs. Aside from being old and heavy, she was lame because her feet had been bound into small triangles since childhood—a deplorable custom that persisted a thousand years until being banned under the Republic. Cook Lao Shen and our rickshaw runner Xiao Chu, with much huffing and puffing, carried her upstairs to the master bedroom. She was only carried downstairs one more time, for a family photo. From the day she arrived, a sitting room upstairs next to her room was converted into a family dining room. All Nainai had to do was to lean on her cane and walk a few steps, to arrive at the dining table for her meals with the rest of the family.

Due to the eight-year war with the Japanese, we had never visited our ancestral home, except for once when I was still a baby. I therefore had no memory of Nainai before she arrived in our Hangzhou home. Needless to say, she and my younger sister Lining had never laid eyes on each other. There was a chasm that neither side tried to bridge. Nainai might have cared for her other sets of grandchildren—children of my father's siblings—who had grown up under her wing, but we were mere strangers to her.

But whenever it was snowy, rainy, or just somewhat windy outside, Nainai would always, as soon as she settled herself down at the breakfast table, tell my mother: "The weather's terrible; shouldn't we keep the children home today?" My mother was on the spot. As a daughter-in-law, she wasn't supposed to go against Nainai's wishes; yet she couldn't let us miss so many days of school. I didn't pay much attention to their exchanges at the time, but years later when I became a mother myself, I really hated to send my children out to brave the cold on those frigid Iowa mornings. It occurred to me then with a sudden pang that maybe Nainai, in her own way, did care for my sister and me after all.

Was Nainai lonely? She was illiterate and did no needlework. Her only pastime was playing mahjongg with relatives—until she became too feeble to sit at the mahjongg table. Other than three times a day for meals, she never left her room. When my parents were home, which was not often, they would pay her a brief visit every morning to inquire about her wellbeing. Of course, the maid Zhongying always chatted with her when she went in her room to clean, to fill her hot water thermos, and to empty her chamber pot. Other than that, Nainai was pretty much left alone.

Sometimes, I could hear her walk about in her room, her cane making a "didu…didu" noise. Other times she would murmur to herself or burp loudly. Nainai had problems with digestion. She always complained that cooked or raw radishes gave her severe heartburn. So did several other foods. You would think she would stay away from them, but she ate her fill just the same. Even after a meal free of offensive foods, she would often lie in bed afterwards moaning loudly: "Ah yoo wei…ahya…ai…my Mama…aai." Her moaning and groaning, tremulous, quavering, went on and on in an endless loop. My skull tingled. And I felt embarrassed for Nainai. Why would she be calling for her long-dead mother when she was so ancient herself? Eventually I learned to tune her out.

On such occasions, when my mother was home, she would go to Nainai's room to see if she was all right. When she reappeared, she would ask Zhongying to prepare a traditional herb medicine soup for Nainai. Zhongying would whisper to Lao Shen about their elderly mistress, "Our *Lao Taitai* overate again."

Everyone in the family knew Nainai loved to eat. Her appetite seemed insatiable. To prevent her from having indigestion, my mother would often signal Zhongying to start clearing the table before Nainai was finished. When my father was home, he would sometimes say, half in jest, "*Niang*, if you don't stop, the servants will have to go hungry tonight."

Last spring—the first spring after Nainai moved in with us—her youngest son, we called him Xiao Shushu, Small Uncle, came to visit her. On *Duanwu* Festival day, Nainai polished off two large *zhong zi*, meat and sticky rice wrapped in bamboo leaves, traditional food for this Festival. When she reached for a third, Small Uncle was quick to intercept: "*Niang*," he said tactfully, "please allow me to eat this one." Nainai put down her chopsticks, visibly miffed.

Back row: Cousin Li, my mother, my father, my father's younger brother (Xiao Shushu), Cousin Paul
Middle row: Me (Annuo), my sister (Lining), and my brother (Charley)
Front row: My maternal grandmother (Wainainai) and paternal grandmother (Nainai)

Even with my older brother Charley away at boarding school, our large, European-style two-storied house was always brimming with people. My father was a gregarious man, who loved nothing more than to be surrounded by friends and relatives. My mother, therefore, was in charge of the logistics of providing good food for the guests—three scrumptious meals a day plus afternoon and midnight snacks.

After the war my father went into the salt business, which required him to spend more time in Shanghai than in our home in Hangzhou. Besides he rather enjoyed the night life Shanghai had to offer, so much so that whenever he came home for his brief stays, he always brought his entourage of Shanghai friends with him.

Whenever they descended on us, both the downstairs and upstairs dining rooms were pressed into service. Most days the two round dining tables, each capable of seating twelve to fourteen, would be full, and we children, including Cousin Li, would have to wait for the guests to finish and leave the tables so that we could eat the leftovers. When there were not enough leftovers, we would wait for our cook Lao Shen, exhausted after turning out elaborate meals all day, to make something quick and easy to feed us—like crab-flavored eggs.

I never minded eating leftovers or the crab-flavored eggs. The eggs were stir-fried in hot oil without being beaten first, and minced fresh ginger, soy sauce, and dark vinegar were added to emulate the flavor of crabs.

Not being seated at the table meant that I could enjoy a relaxed meal, without having to put on a smile and address those unfamiliar and unknowable adults politely as uncles and aunts. They obviously took no interest in me, although a few pretended to. I, in turn, didn't like the way they talked, couldn't understand why these so-called grownups had so many empty, stupid things to say, or why they said them as if they were imparting profound, earth-shaking insights. I also grew disgusted at the women who giggled flirtatiously and pretended to be, oh, so friendly to one another. I was twelve years old, no longer a child, and had grown used to immersing myself in my own world, observing the guests with cold detachment.

My detachment, however, often dissolved after dinner. After hanging around all day, playing mahjongg and eating and drinking their fill, many of my father's guests would get "itchy feet."

Our rickshaw runner Xiao Chu would be summoned to spread talc powder on the floor in the large front hall. Some eager friend would crank the gramophone, and popular songs like "Let the Champagne Flow," "Climbing Roses Are Blossoming Every Where," and "When Will You Return to Me?" would be played. Excitement would stir, permeating the air.

Even though my mother always reminded my sister and me to go to bed early so as to be ready for school the next day, we couldn't resist the temptation to tiptoe down, hide ourselves at the turn of the stairs and peek at the goings on.

It was an astonishing sight. Everyone knew the rule handed down from Confucius' time that members of the opposite sex are not supposed to touch. These grownups, including my parents, who normally seemed to follow this rule religiously, openly held hands on such occasions. More amazing, the man's right hand held—of all things—a woman's waist while the woman, giggling, placed her left hand on his shoulder. She merrily, if not dreamily, slid on the slick floor to the rhythm of the music, "bon—cha—cha, bon—cha—cha." In these instances, my sister and I would exchange glances, not knowing what to make of the unbelievable scene.

Uncle Zhang was the best dancer among the guests, and he loved a type of dance called the tango. The mysterious Western tango music seemed to stop momentarily prior to advancing, while Uncle Zhang and his dancing partner's steps repelled, then welcomed each other's attentions. The tango never failed to reveal something mysterious and inviting of the adult world and bring out some vague, unspeakable, incomprehensible desire in the innermost reaches of my heart.

Then came a day when our father actually summoned us to teach us to dance and join his friends. His close friend and schoolmate Ren Xianqun had been appointed mayor of Hangzhou and was staying in our house until his wife and children could join him. He loved to dance, but as the newly appointed mayor, a high-profile civil servant, he could not visit dance halls where girls were on call as "taxi dancers." Imagine the scandal if reporters should spot him. So my father came up with the solution of having my younger sister and me fill in as temporary dancing partners. We caught on quickly and enjoyed ourselves thoroughly, even danced the tango with Uncle Zhang. But there was a downside: "the itchy feet syndrome" was contagious. From then on, we would get an irresistible urge to dance whenever we heard popular music, but were strictly forbidden by our father to do so, even in our college years.

At the time, though, I would glow with excitement and would rush upstairs afterward to describe everything in detail to Cousin Li—skipping, of course, the part about my own reactions about the tango. Cousin Li, who could always be found in his room studying under a lamp, would furrow his eyebrows while shaking his head in a sigh: "You girls…" His smile, indulgent and indifferent at the same time, showed that nothing in the world could disturb his calm. It made me feel childish. No matter how hard I tried, I always felt hopelessly immature compared to Cousin Li.

Cousin Li had joined our household with his father, Da Jiu, Big Uncle (my mother's eldest brother), and his paternal grandmother, my maternal grandmother, Wainainai. The word *Wai* literally means "outside." So now we had an *inside* grandmother and an *outside* grandmother. The three arrived shortly after Nainai. For as long as I could remember, relatives had flowed in and out of our house, sometimes staying for months, but most of them were from *inside*. This time was an exception.

The original intent of my parents was probably to bring

Wainainai, my maternal grandmother, on the terrace of our Hangzhou home.

Wainainai here to keep Nainai company. If that had been their motive, they must have been terribly disappointed. It was true that the two had something in common. They were about the same age, they dressed in similar dark-colored, short mandarin jackets and long Chinese-style pants, and combed their sparse, white hair neatly into a bun at the back of their heads. Both were illiterate and had bound feet.

But they were from different provinces and spoke different dialects. And they had never met before even though my parents had been married for more than sixteen years.

They were a study in contrasts. Nainai was tall and heavy. Wainainai was short and stout. Nainai could hardly walk, whereas Wainainai was energetic, going up and downstairs with ease; her bound feet never slowed her down at all. She loved to spend time outdoors in the countryside, digging for edible weeds or in the garden planting fava beans, peas and other vegetables. Nainai was a meat-eating Catholic. Wainainai was a Buddhist who refrained from eating meat on the first and fifteenth of every month in the lunar calendar and enjoyed drinking a small cup or two of warmed Shaoxing wine in the late afternoon.

They never became friends. Carefully staying away from each other, they fulfilled the Chinese saying: *River water doesn't interfere with well water.* Was it because Wainainai felt uncomfortable? Although times had changed, it was still unusual to live in the house of one's son-in-law, especially when Wainainai had to bring her son and grandson with her.

Cousin Li was Da Jiu's only son. Da Jiu's wife had died early. Foot loose and fancy free by nature, Da Jiu refused to be tied down by a young son. Preferring a life of pleasure, he didn't want to take care of his aging mother either. Before the war, he had played mahjongg and lived, on a long-term basis, in the most expensive brothel in Shanghai, where he spent my maternal grandfather's fortune in no time at all. When the war started, Wainainai had to abandon her ancestral home and take Cousin Li, her grandson of not quite 10 years old, to live with her number-three son and daughter-in-law in the interior of China.

My mother said that her sister-in-law, Cousin Li's aunt, used the child like a servant—she made him work after school taking care of her own little boys and doing other household chores. The aunt also loved to punish him by forbidding him to eat dinner. Many a night he went to bed hungry. Wainainai was powerless to protect him although he was her oldest grandson. She and my mother both believed that was why Cousin Li was so thin and malnourished.

Perhaps those years of pain and suffering under his aunt's roof formed Cousin Li's obstinate and taciturn personality and his angular, resolute facial features. His thin lips were always tightly shut as if to hold his anger firmly in check. His neck, Adam's apple already showing, was stiff and straight. His body, gowned in cotton, dark blue in winter, light blue in summer, was slim and upright. When he stood he was motionless, and when he walked he was noiseless.

After the three of them arrived, I was no longer bored, not even on weekends. I started following Wainainai to the backyard to dig bamboo shoots, or to the countryside near our house to dig *jicai* or pick *caodou*. Wainainai loved to stir fry *caodou*. Just before taking it out of the wok, she would spray some wine on it. It was the most delicious vegetable I had ever tasted, not that I had ever been much of a vegetable lover.

After the spring rains, numerous gray-brownish-colored *di-er*, "earth ears," a type of fungus like wood ear, would shoot up around the trees and the ground in the yard. Wainainai would gather them to add to the soups or stir fry with vegetables. Their tender, smooth texture and delicate taste gave the dishes a unique dimension.

But shortly after they arrived, I detected something wrong between Da Jiu and Cousin Li. The father and son never seemed to speak to each other. When they appeared in the same room, the air grew thicker, heavier—downright stultifying.

Cousin Li was five years older than me; I was told to address him as Elder Cousin Li. By and by he became just Cousin Li. Once we were better acquainted, I couldn't resist asking him why he had nothing to say to his father. Cousin Li furrowed his brows tightly and gave no reply. When pressed, he responded with words that seemed to come from his nose, "I'm not a girl. Do you want me to do something to get *his* attention?"

Da Jiu seemed to like *me*, however. He was eager to teach me Tang poetry, patiently explaining the Chinese equivalent of the iambic pentameter: "ping ping ze ze ze ping ping." But I couldn't keep my mind on what he said. What I really wanted to ask him but could not bring myself to say was, *Why don't you teach your own son? What's wrong between you two?*

Owing to my anger at Da Jiu, I managed to learn nothing from the poetry he tried to teach me, but on the occasions Da Jiu the gourmet made crab bisque, beef bone marrow soup with "egg skins" (thin egg noodles made with lots of eggs and a little flour), and *jicai* meat balls, I would follow him to the kitchen, fascinated. Only Cousin Li remained an outsider, uninterested in anything involving his father.

At the end of the first semester, the reticent Cousin Li surprised everybody: he came home with a prize and a plaque for winning the Chinese Chess Championship. Nobody had ever seen him play chess or any other table games. Later I discovered that he had won all the Chinese chess competitions since elementary school.

From that moment on, I kept pestering him to teach me the game. He finally gave in by starting me on simpler ones—Chinese checkers and *wuzi* chess. It turned out he was a wizard at every kind of game. Even our maid Zhongying was impressed. She would often tell me, "Your Cousin Li is truly talented but he never shows off. Not like you. If you did anything, you'd want the whole world to know about it."

I didn't disagree with Zhongying, but I found her choice of words disagreeable. In fact, she was getting more and more tiresome. Many times when she got my bathwater ready, and tried to stay and scrub my back just like before, I would push her out. But she lingered outside the door, complaining in a loud voice, "I'm just afraid you won't get yourself clean!" I was furious. Even though she had worked for us all these years, she didn't need to holler like that, making everyone in the house believe I wasn't capable of bathing myself.

That year not only did the magnolia bloom early, but summer came in a hurry. By mid-June, it was already hot as July, and July itself was scorching. My father left early for Shanghai, his entourage of friends disappearing with him. Shortly after, at the invitation of their rich cousin—our Seventh Uncle, as we called him, because he was number seven in his family—my mother and Da Jiu went to Lu Shan, the famous mountain resort area where all the bigwigs, including President Chiang Kai-shek, spent their summers. My brother Charley went on a boarding school summer field trip. With only two grandmothers and three youngsters left, the house became unusually quiet.

But I didn't mind; I felt wonderfully free that summer. Although my case of diphtheria again reared its ugly head, and I was told by doctors to stay home for the coming school year, I still had to keep up with my summer homework. But all I needed to do was to spend half an hour each morning practicing my calligraphy and filling a page for my weekly journal. The rest of the time I was free to do anything I pleased, without having to behave the way my parents thought I should, or worrying about having done something they thought I shouldn't.

And most importantly, I was proud that after months of practice, I had made tremendous progress in Chinese chess.

Cousin Li, no match for my insistence, had finally let me graduate from Chinese checkers and *Wuzi* chess, and started teaching me Chinese chess, or *xiangqi*. In anticipation of my weakness, he laid down one cardinal rule at the outset: *luo zi bu hui*. A piece, once down on the board, could not be retracted.

In the beginning, he would allow me one chariot, two horses, and two cannons. Using a single remaining chariot, he managed to win in a few minutes. Even soldier pieces, which could only go forward one step at a time, and could take side steps only after crossing the river, grew ferocious under Cousin Li.

At first I got angry, then I cried "Unfair!" But in the end I had to admit that he always won fair and square. He seemed to be prescient, able to see through my intentions when I picked up my piece: "Don't be greedy now, thinking you can take my elephant. Once you do, look—I'll be able to check-mate you."

He was already prepared for my moves. I accused him of being sly—a crafty, tricky old scoundrel. He didn't mind. "If you don't think ahead and just do whatever you please when you make a move, how will you improve?"

Over time, having heard too many times his warning: *one wrong move can cost you the whole game*, I learned to temper my impulsive nature and tried to use my head instead.

Gradually, ever so slowly, Cousin Li had to work a bit harder. Because I hated to lose and harbored the hope that one of these days we could at least have a draw, I became more and more careful when making my moves. I kept reminding myself of the old proverb, *Think three times before you act*, and ended up deliberating a thousand times. I would think and think and think some more. I never wanted to make a wrong move. Sometimes when my fingers were on a piece, I didn't dare pick it up. Other times I held the piece in my hand, but was too afraid to put it down on the board.

I took so much time that Cousin Li tried to speed me up, "Hey, how long are you going to think about this? Are you going to play or not? I don't have all day to wait for you to make a move." But he said it with a nice smile and sat like a rock, motionless.

One afternoon I was sweating over my next move as usual. As always, my hands were not idle—I was waving a fan with my left, spooning sugared fresh tomato into my mouth with my right. It occurred to me how weird it was that hot temperatures never seemed to bother Cousin Li. He was always cool and calm, an irritating sight indeed.

All of a sudden Zhongying appeared at my side and said in a low voice, "Would you like to go and look in on *Lao taitai*? She seems to be having great pains this time."

By now I was so good at tuning her out that I wasn't bothered by Nainai's groans. But Zhongying was right. Her moaning "My...Mama...ai" was different from before. Each time it sounded a little more desperate than the last. The night before, Nainai had eaten a lot of diced pork stir fried with pickled cucumber, fresh bamboo shoots and green soybeans, and had started moaning shortly after going back to her room.

"Doesn't she always feel better after a bowl of herbal soup?"

"Aiya, my dear Miss! I already gave her the soup three times. It didn't help a bit. Your Wainainai just looked in on her; she doesn't know what to do."

I had no idea either, but I was almost giddy with pride. For the first time she had approached me as though I were a grown up—one who was worth consulting on important matters. I abandoned my game and sugar-marinated tomatoes and followed Zhongying to Nainai's room.

Nainai's face was gray and sallow. Her eyes opened only a tiny slit. Her old-fashioned, ivory-white linen pajamas looked more like preserved cabbage from having been rubbed all night on the thin straw mat on the bed. She smelled of sweat and decay. My confidence and giddiness dissipated instantly. I felt helpless, but Zhongying was pushing me toward Nainai's bed, speaking loudly, "*Lao Taitai*, look who's here to see you?" Nainai's murky eyes opened and looked at me for a moment and closed right away, but her moaning continued.

"Do you think we should call your mother?"

Zhongying said these words in a whisper, but they brought immediate reaction from Nainai, who waved her hand weakly and spoke in a low and indistinct voice, "I'm... all right... Rest...ah-yoo...couple of...days...I'll be...well."

Although my mother left us Seventh Uncle's resort telephone number, I had never called her. I had never called anyone on the phone. In fact, I was afraid to talk on the phone. But my mother always called home every few days. Usually Zhongying answered the phone, gave a brief report, and quickly hung up. Sometimes Lining wanted to talk to our mother, but Zhongying would always cut her short,

"Fine, fine, that's enough." I couldn't remember when my mother had last called.

Rummaging around the house, Cousin Li managed to find a medical book. The two of us sat side by side studying it, wrestling with unfamiliar vocabulary. Nainai's symptoms were like those of acute appendicitis, and similar to the ones for typhus. Both diseases sounded serious. But what if we were wrong? If my mother rushed home all the way from Lu Shan, and Nainai turned out to be fine, wouldn't *I* be blamed for sounding the false alarm? But what if it was really serious? Cousin Li seemed to be mulling over the possibilities, and the decisive and capable Zhongying was obviously at a loss.

I was on pins and needles the rest of the afternoon. At dinnertime, listening to Nainai's moaning in the next room, I hardly knew what I was eating. Only Lining was in high spirits. For once I envied her childishness. She was free from the worry of whether to make a call after dinner.

Thank heavens, before the dishes were cleared away, my mother called and decided immediately that she would leave first thing in the morning for home. I was able to heave a huge sigh of relief.

Little did I know that the days waiting for my mother to return would turn out to be no less agonizing. Nainai could no longer get out of bed, her moaning becoming weaker and weaker. She used to have such great appetite, now she couldn't eat a thing. Zhongying tried her best to get her to swallow some thin porridge without success. Although Wainainai and Nainai didn't usually have much to do with each other, now Wainainai was concerned. Several times she went to Nainai's room to see her and emerged looking somber and sad.

My mother arrived in the late afternoon of the second day. She took one look at Nainai and arranged for an ambulance. Nainai was taken to the hospital around dusk. When her stretcher was carried downstairs, her eyes were closed tightly. Her cheekbones protruded, and her skin was dry, loose and yellow. The turnaround of the stairs was too narrow; half of the stretcher stuck out of the window. For a few moments Nainai's bound feet shook violently on the stretcher before coming inside the window again. Finally, she disappeared from view.

Early next morning the hospital called. Nainai had worsened overnight and died at dawn. My mother immediately left for the hospital. In the afternoon, Xiao Chu was sent back with the family rickshaw to take me to the hospital.

I was scared. Learning about Nainai's passing made my brain numb. I was squeamish about death. In the Children's Hospital when my roommate died, I turned my face to the wall to avoid looking into the boy's dead face. The second and last time I had encountered death, our doorman Lao Lee, who had last-stage tuberculosis, was taken to the hospital late one night and never came back. I heard that he was cremated.

Nainai died all by herself. Was she scared when the king of the underworld, *Yanluowang*, sent his fearsome guardians *Ox-Head* and *Horse-Face* to snatch her away? Without family at her side, if something untoward happened to her, she could rise as a *stiff corpse* to harm people. Then what would we do? I was beset with all types of troubling questions, but couldn't bring myself to ask anyone, not even Cousin Li. And I needed the answers urgently. I ended up doing it in a roundabout way, asking Cousin Li if he had ever seen dead people. Plenty during the war, he replied. "When people die they are gone. Just *poof*, like a lamp goes out. No big deal." Then how about ghosts? Cousin Li expelled air through his nose, "Ghosts are stories grownups make up to scare kids. I, for one, have never seen any ghosts."

Though I believed Cousin Li, I avoided looking toward the bed when I stepped into Nainai's hospital room—and encountered an unbelievable scene.

I didn't know that my father had come back from Shanghai. My tall, gracious, and confident father, always full of good humor, was now acting like a spoiled child throwing a huge temper tantrum, thumping his chest and stamping his feet, crying his heart out. It was strange—my father was never an important part of my life, but when he behaved so abnormally, he flipped my world upside down. I felt like a passenger of a little boat capsizing in a big storm.

As I stood confused, mesmerized, my father suddenly thrust his angry, twisted face in front of me. "Did you see your Nainai? You haven't even shed a single tear. Are you a human being? *Are you?*" The violence of my father's anger and upbraiding shocked me. "Waw…" Frightened, I started to cry.

I heard my mother say, "She's just going to be in the way. Why don't we let Xiao Chu take her back when Zhongying gets here?" But my father shook his head, mumbling something about the proper protocol of family presence. I had never heard the word *protocol* before, but my heart sank. If Lining had been here, I thought, would she have behaved any better? Why was she always so lucky, picking today of all days to run a fever?

Zhongying finally arrived, carrying a large red-silk bundle. As soon as she put down the bundle, not bothering to wipe the sweat off her face, she set to work with my mother as though they had prior understanding. They started giving

Nainai a sponge bath! Eyes and mouth half open, Nainai was like a rag doll, with her wrinkled arms, legs, torso, long, hanging breasts and private parts shamelessly on view.

Cousin Li was wrong. Dying was much more horrifying than a light going out. Nainai alive was never so eerily quiet and still, so thoroughly indifferent and unfeeling about what was done to her or going on around her, or so otherworldly and spooky. Though the room was stiflingly hot, chills were creeping up my spine.

Like a magic trick, my mother opened the red-silk bundle and shook out layer upon layer—tidily folded in squares—of various articles of clothing, made of silk, satin, and brocade, in the brightest, most lustrous colors imaginable—pink, red, purple, gold, emerald green, and royal blue, to name some. There were underwear, short mandarin jackets, long skirts, and long gowns. The outerwear was elaborately embroidered with flowers, birds or words like "long life" and "good fortune." These, I realized, must have been Nainai's funeral clothes, custom-made years ahead for this very eventuality.

Together they slid on the intricate clothing—supposedly the more layers, the better—over Nainai's body, stiff and yellow. The rich and resplendent covered the ugly and hideous: lush, eye-dazzling colors and shiny, smooth fabrics over Nainai's wrinkles and age spots. What cruel contrast!

While they continued with their work, I never stopped crying, but not a single drop of my tears that afternoon was shed from grief for Nainai. Only *I* knew in my heart that my sobbing was from *terror*. My father was right. I was subhuman.

My chills started as soon as I got home. When Zhongying saw my flushed face and put her hand on my forehead to see if I was running a fever, I recoiled, screaming shrilly, "Don't you touch me!"

Those same hands had just scrubbed a dead body!

I couldn't eat dinner and was sent to bed early. I felt dizzy. My head was swelling. A curtain seemed to have descended, separating me from the rest of the world.

In my twilight state I followed a crowd to a deserted area in the countryside. Someone told me it was Nainai's cremation site. Sure enough, Nainai in her bright multi-colored finery was lying on a stretcher in the center of the lot. But where did everybody go? I wanted to chase after them, but was rooted to the spot and couldn't move, watching helplessly as the fire danced closer and closer to Nainai. She didn't move. I tried to call out, to warn her, but my voice failed me. The tongue of fire quickly licked her "long-life clothes," the proper clothes to meet *Yanluowang*, the king of the underworld. Layers and layers, red, purple, gold, green and blue silk lifting and disappearing, lifting and disappearing, when Nainai suddenly sat up, stiff as a board…

"Ah…Ah…" Terrified, I screamed out loud and saw that *I* had sat up. In the next room my father snored rhythmically. Outside my window the night was pitch dark.

I was sick for weeks. I missed Nainai's funeral and burial. If not for the nightmares every night, I would have counted myself lucky.

When I finally recovered, it was autumn. Although I was not supposed to go to school that year, I was allowed to show up for one day to hand in my summer homework. That fall, the civil war, which had started as soon as the eight-year Sino-Japanese war ended three years ago, took a definite turn for the worse. It looked as if the Nationalists were not going to be able to hold on to the mainland. When grownups got together, all they could talk or argue about was whether to leave or stay. In my school, the student body had shrunk noticeably. Some students left with family for the countryside to escape the coming upheaval; others moved to Taiwan, Hong Kong, or abroad. My seatmate told me in a whisper that her family was leaving for Taiwan soon.

Taiwan, that faraway, previously unheard of place, had acquired great importance overnight. My mother's rich cousin, our Seventh Uncle, the one who owned a summer resort in Lu Shan, flew to Taiwan to see if he should move his factory and family there. But he only stayed three days before flying back to Shanghai and never mentioned moving to Taiwan again—he couldn't stand the poverty and backwardness.

He described the streets in Taipei: "There were no cars, not even street lights at night. All you could hear was 'ba—da, ba—da,' noises made by men and women walking in Japanese wooden clogs with thong toes, no socks. The women's legs, covered by mosquito bites, looked like red-bean popsicles!" And he added with great feeling, "The houses didn't even have flush toilets—you had to squat over a stinky hole in the floor. What kind of life is that?"

My father returned to Shanghai soon after Nainai's burial. After the Mid-Autumn Festival, Da Jiu accompanied Wainainai, who steadfastly refused to go to Taiwan, to Shanghai to stay with her youngest daughter, our aunt Yiniang. A few days after Da Jiu came back, Cousin Li moved into his school dormitory. The house grew quiet, and my mother, weighed down by the gravity of the coming change, started sorting things in the house.

Before Cousin Li left, I walked into my mother's room one day and found her staring at stuff spread all over the place. I gathered my courage, assumed the casual tone of a grownup, and asked,

"So when are we leaving?"

My mother replied, "I don't know for sure yet. Your father is trying to get tickets. It's not going to be long now."

I was shaken. It was true then; we were really leaving, going to that backwater Taiwan.

"And leave Cousin Li here all by himself?" As soon as these words were out, I froze, for I realized it wasn't appropriate for me to talk that way to my mother.

Mother seemed to be ready for me, though—she put down the things in her hand. "Cousin Li is Da Jiu's son, and Da Jiu doesn't plan to leave. How can we take him with us?"

I wanted to say, *You know Da Jiu doesn't care about him. If we leave, he will be all alone. What is he going to do?* But I couldn't quite say it. I didn't mean to cry; the last thing I wanted was to appear childish, but tears came just the same.

My mother, unsurprised, continued, "You are no longer a little girl. You'll be fourteen after the New Year. In your Wainainai's generation, a girl your age would be almost ready to get married. So stop acting like a child; try to understand that every person has his own life, his own destiny. Cousin Li can't be with us forever. Besides," she changed her tune, "although he will be staying at the dorm, it won't be very different from living here. Zhongying will go and visit him and take care of him. We *are* leaving, but chances are, in six months, maybe a year, we'll be back…"

Ah—Zhongying, who had been with us for many years, would be staying, and she would take care of Cousin Li. Six months, at most a year, we would be back. Life would be the same as before. So going to Taiwan was not as tragic, or final as I thought. I felt much relieved and started to imagine

Cousin Li's smile when I saw him again, and played Chinese chess with him again. One of these days I might even beat him in a game. Then a thought struck me—what if Cousin Li had a girlfriend by then and wouldn't want to play Chinese chess with me any more? I shook my head and banished the unpleasant thought from my mind.

Zhongying and Da Jiu saw us off the morning we left. The four of us took only three suitcases. Everything in the house was kept as it was, waiting for our return.

The train was unbelievably crowded. A trip that was usually a four-and-a-half-hour ride took a whole day. We arrived in Shanghai after dinnertime, met up with Father, and boarded a plane before dawn.

In Taipei, we moved into a tiny Japanese house, literally with nothing except four walls. Doors were made of translucent white paper that could be poked through by a two-year-old, and floors were covered with large, thick straw mats called *tatami*—on which we slept.

For the first time in her life, my mother had to carry a basket to the market to shop for food. There was no kitchen in the house. For meals she squatted on the floor of the only hallway outside the living room, hunching her back to make fire in a small coal stove. At first the rice was burned at the bottom and raw on top. Gradually she got the hang of it.

What my mother couldn't get used to was having no furniture. Sitting on *tatami* made her legs so sore and numb she could hardly stand up. But my father said, so what? The Japanese did that all their lives. I understood what he meant. We would make do for a few months, because we were going home soon. *Going home* seemed to be everybody's wish, what we thought about day and night, but nobody dared to mention.

Every morning my father made his rounds of friends' houses for news from the mainland. One day on his way home, he bought a whole set of wicker furniture. When the pieces were delivered, everyone was overjoyed. Charley, Lining, and I copied our parents, sinking our bodies into the soft cushions of the wicker sofas. It was too comfortable for words! At the same time a moment of clarity washed over me: we were not going home any time soon.

Zhongying chose not to go with us to Taiwan, but was willing to stay to take care of our house. After we left, she paid for someone to write several letters to let us know things were fine at home. Then a letter arrived informing us that Da Jiu had left for an unknown destination. There was no telling when he would be back. Another reported that Cousin Li had contracted mild tuberculosis. She had gone to his dorm several times to bring him food.

Cousin Li also wrote to my parents a few times to inquire after their wellbeing. His letters were brief, with never a word about his sickness. One letter even said that now the Communists were in power, the poor finally would have a better life.

But not long after, a letter from Zhongying reported that Cousin Li's tuberculosis had abruptly worsened. He died shortly after. Soon after, the so-called Bamboo Curtain descended—communication between the Chinese mainland and Taiwan was completely cut off. We never learned what happened to Zhongying or our house.

My parents shared the contents of these letters with us in a cursory manner. After all, what could they have done? They were so far away. I reacted the same way: I sighed a little and never mentioned any of them. We ourselves had many more important, more urgent matters in our lives to worry about. My father found a job; he was busy with work and social activities. Our Small Uncle—Father's younger brother—came from Chongqing with his wife and our cousins Paul and Cecilia, and stayed with us. We moved into a large Japanese house, complete with kitchen and bathroom. We were busy adjusting to school, carrying our Japanese bento box lunches every morning. Forbidden to learn to ride a bicycle, I had to take the city bus to school. The buses were notoriously crowded in Taipei, and nobody stood in line.

Nainai and her funeral clothes finally faded from my dreams, and Cousin Li never appeared in any of them.

One day when I came home from school, I was surprised to see Da Jiu sitting in our living room. He had somehow managed to escape to Hong Kong and had discovered our whereabouts in Taiwan. After he found a job and settled in our house, he was enthusiastic about cooking again. Since not all the ingredients he needed were available in Taiwan, he had to settle for making his excellent fish bisque.

Did my mother ever talk with Da Jiu about his son's untimely death? I didn't know. Anyhow it was probably irrelevant. Da Jiu never mentioned Cousin Li, and we were thoughtful enough to stay mum on the subject. Cousin Li therefore was thoroughly forgotten by his family, as if he had never existed, never lived among us.

After getting my university degree, I left for the States for graduate school, got married, and stayed. Several decades went by. Some people like to say that the dead survive in the memory of the living. When Nainai died I had felt no sorrow, but when the magnolia bloomed each spring, it would remind me of her excitement—when she hooked the magnolia branches through the window with her cane.

Yet I rarely thought of Cousin Li. Nor did I ever play Chinese chess again. Maybe it was Cousin Li's karma. He simply failed to make deep connections with people.

But occasionally—once in a great while—when I fell into a pensive mood, I would ponder: If blood is thicker than water, why did I feel nothing but fear with Nainai's passing? If I had cared for Cousin Li and had shared his joys and pains, how could I have been so unfeeling about his death? I was puzzled and guilt-ridden.

Until one day when I had tea with an American friend. We were talking about similarities and dissimilarities in our respective cultures when suddenly, my friend asked, "You often mention the term *jiajiao*—family discipline. Is Chinese family discipline so powerful? When you were a child, did *jiajiao* control your emotions? Your happiness, anger, and sadness?"

They say one can get intoxicated from too much tea. So maybe I was inebriated by herbal tea that day. Perhaps it was my friend's caring tone of voice, her particular questions, or her background as a psychotherapist. Or was it the soulfulness and sorrow of the last touch of sunshine in that winter afternoon?

Something triggered my memory of Cousin Li, long buried in my heart. His kind smile when he taught me Chinese chess, his stubborn silence in front of his father. The images flashed before me with such clarity. How much pain and anger was locked behind his firmly closed lips! Eighteen years old, still an adolescent, he had died alone, indeed like a light going out, gone from the world without a trace...

Before I realized it, my long-held tears burst forth, rushing down my face without a sound.

EIGHT

Epilogue

1949-

My father was the only one among his friends and relatives who had fought the Japanese under the Nationalists and been attacked by the Communists. If the six years he spent risking his own and his family's lives taught him anything, it was a deep distrust of the Communists. Before we fled to Taiwan, he tried his utmost to persuade his friends and relatives to leave, too. He was a persuasive man. My mother used to say he could talk a dead man alive. But he failed to talk any of our relatives into making the move. Staying close to one's roots had always been an important—if not the most important—part of Chinese culture. Our relatives probably also felt that they were in less danger from the Communists; my father's wartime experiences might render him a prime target for the firing squad or worse, but they had always been obedient citizens. They had never offended anyone in power. Like countless others who chose to stay, they reasoned: "We survived under the Japanese. The Communists are our fellow countrymen, like brothers born from the same mother. What will they do to us? What *can* they do?"

While my father was right about leaving, however, he was mistaken about the timing. Like millions of others, he didn't anticipate that the Nationalists would lose the war so soon. Our departure for Taiwan was so precipitous that he left behind shiploads of salt—his livelihood—and had to borrow money from his former superior and later close friend Han to survive, when we first arrived in Taiwan.

He was also wrong in thinking we would return home in short order. Millions of others thought the same way. The last words families and friends said to one another were: "See you soon." Sadly, it was not to be. Within less than a year the Communists had taken over, and across the Taiwan Strait, the drumbeat of the slogan *Blood Wash Taiwan* could be heard from one end of the mainland to the other.

While we were still living in that first tiny Japanese house with no kitchen, my father's younger brother, Xiao Shushu (Small Paternal Uncle), who had visited Nainai in Hangzhou (standing next to my father in the family photo), left Chongqing at the last moment and arrived in Taiwan.

Chongqing, the former wartime capital, had become the capital of China again as the Nationalists lost more and more territory to the Communists. For years Xiao Shushu had made his home in Chongqing and owned a pharmaceutical factory there. Despite my father's urgent letters, he chose to stay. However, on September 2, 1949, less than a month before the Communists' total victory, my uncle became thoroughly frightened by a disastrous fire in Chongqing's waterfront and banking district, which burned for 18 hours, killing nearly 3,000 people and injured 10,000. It's on record as one of the world's worst fires. The two warring parties pointed the finger at each other. For days after his arrival, all our uncle could talk about was the fire, and he would get all red in the face. He had to leave his pharmaceutical factory behind, but managed to bring his wife and our cousins Paul and Cecilia—children of our father's older sister, Wu Niangniang. (Paul had lived with us in Hangzhou until leaving for Chongqing to attend college.) The four of them lived with us for many years.

The immediate impact was that we had to move to a bigger house. Soon after, our two maternal uncles joined us via Hong Kong; first Da Jiu (Cousin Li's father) showed up one day, then Si Jiu, our fourth maternal uncle, appeared with his wife and five-year-old daughter. Our new house was so crowded that we slept several to a room. For a long time, my brother slept on top of a trunk; later he made his bed on the living room floor. For years, Cousin Cecilia, my sister Lining, and I shared the same bed.

Every morning, our cook would make a giant wok of egg fried rice to feed our brood of thirteen. To save money, only one egg was used: a duck egg, cheaper and larger than a chicken egg. In the morning I always searched for that bit of yellow in my fried rice, but in vain.

That experience taught me to treat eggs with respect for the rest of my life. Though eggs here are cheap and my cholesterol count high, I have never been able to bring myself to throw away a single egg yolk.

After abandoning our hopes of returning to the mainland, we began to live under daily threat of a Communist invasion of Taiwan. My father declared to us many times:

"We will all throw ourselves into the ocean if the Communists come here."

We knew it was not hyperbole; he meant every word of it. He would have pushed us in then jumped in after us.

However, life is full of ironies. Our years in Taiwan turned out to be the most peaceful we had known. What saved us was the Korean War. The Americans needed Taiwan for its strategic location, and a mutual defense treaty was signed to protect Taiwan from "Red China," as it was called at the time.

Still, to avoid the possible fate of all of us drowning in the ocean, my father sent his children and our cousins one by one to the States, borrowing money to do so. He and my mother stayed in Taiwan, where my father enjoyed a successful career building up Taiwan's fisheries industry, until they came to the States to retire in 1989. For most of my parents' 40 years in Taiwan they largely enjoyed the same gregarious lifestyle they had briefly had in Shanghai when they were first married, and later in Hangzhou after the Sino-Japanese War.

In fact, those of our relatives who managed to escape to Taiwan lived a normal, peaceful life. Da Jiu lived with us for many years and worked for the Taiwan Provincial Shipping Bureau. Si Jiu, his wife and daughter stayed with us for a few years until they found their own quarters. They had another daughter, and the whole family emigrated to New York. Xiao Shushu and his wife eventually settled in Toronto, Canada.

For 30 years after we fled to Taiwan in January 1949, the Bamboo Curtain—the Chinese equivalent of the Soviet Iron Curtain—prevented us from communicating with anyone on the mainland. We had no idea what happened to our relatives and friends there. While the bitter cold war since 1949 between the Chinese mainland and Taiwan remained unrelenting, however, the political situation in the U.S. began to change. As National Security Advisor, Henry Kissinger made two trips to China in 1971, paving the way for President Nixon's historic visit to China in 1972.

Da Jiu in his later years in Taiwan

Following Nixon's visit, China started buying grain from the U.S. to the tune of millions of tons per year. Liaison offices were quickly established, and various unofficial exchanges ensued. The Bamboo Curtain finally opened a crack to the Western world.

At that time, my brother Charley was working for the U.S. Department of Agriculture as the Communist-Asia Area Leader in agricultural economics.

In September 1978, at the invitation of the agricultural officer of the American liaison office in Beijing, Charley made his first visit to China. He spent three weeks in the country visiting different provincial agricultural bureaus to monitor agricultural output in order to gauge the demand for the coming year. Then he went to Shanghai for four days.

At each stop, the local agricultural bureau provided him with a car, a driver, and a guide. Shanghai was no exception.

He had not been in Shanghai since 1945, but he remembered almost all the addresses of places we had lived in—as well as that of our favorite aunt, Yiniang, our mother's younger sister. All the street names in the former French Concession had been changed to expunge its colonial past. The Rue de Pétain had become Hengshan Road, for instance, but the guide still remembered what they had been called before. Along with the names, the street numbers of some of our former abodes had changed also, but Charley, blessed with the memory of an elephant, could still identify the buildings. Unaltered, they had become decrepit with age, like all the other buildings he saw in China during that trip.

At last Charley stood on the sidewalk outside the wrought iron fence, gazing at the second-to-last house on the left in Alley 198—Yiniang and Shushu's three-story home where he had spent many happy days playing childish pranks and riding a tricycle outside. Were they dead or alive? Did they still live there? If so, at that very moment, they could be inside, going about their lives unaware of his presence. The alley was quiet; nobody went in or out. Time seemed to have stood still.

This was merely two years after the Cultural Revolution; the atmosphere in the country was

My brother Charley in his 30's

still tense. He knew his hotel rooms were bugged. He knew that someone would search his belongings each time he left his room. In fact, as he was standing outside the alley gazing longingly at Yiniang's house, a middle-aged woman who looked like a cadre of the neighborhood committee came over demanding to know what he was doing there. He quickly made an excuse and left.

Less than a week after he returned home, he was called to do a briefing on Thursday at 5 p.m. for the Secretary of Agriculture, Robert Bergland. After the briefing, Bergland decided to add Charley to his delegation traveling to China the following week. After receiving a positive response from the Chinese government, my brother found himself on a plane bound for China Tuesday morning.

This time the Chinese Agricultural Minister's interpreter —a woman from Shanghai—discovered that the only ethnic Chinese in Bergland's delegation had a relative in Shanghai. The following morning the Shanghai Agricultural Bureau informed Charley that they had located his aunt and would bring her that evening at 8 p.m. for a reunion. He was told that the appointment was made despite our aunt's protest that she did not wish to see him.

That was how he learned that Yiniang was alive, after 30 long years.

After dinner, the rest of the U. S. Department of Agriculture delegation left for an acrobatic performance at a Shanghai theater. Charley sat alone in his suite in the government guesthouse for VIPs, waiting for our aunt. He was excited—wait till my parents in Taiwan hear about this! He was also anxious. It seemed surreal to be able to see Yiniang face to face and learn what had happened to

Yiniang, holding her youngest daughter Xiaochun, and my mother, in 1948, shortly before we left mainland China for Taiwan

her and Shushu and our extended family. Thirty years. An estimated 77 million Chinese had perished as a result of Chinese Communist rule. Through the prism of news reports, we knew that our relatives must have suffered a great deal on account of their *overseas connection*—that is, their unforgivable crime of being related to those of us who had fled to Taiwan. Unlike our mother, Yiniang had always lived a sheltered life; she was never brave or stoic. She had refused to see my brother, declaring that she had not been in contact with him or his family for 30 years—a desperate protest of innocence. She must have been frightened. And there was no mention of Shushu, Yiniang's husband. What had happened to him?

Charley didn't know what to expect.

When he answered the door, he saw she was not alone. Instead of Shushu, her only son, our Cousin Xiaoming, and the cadre from the Shanghai Agricultural Bureau accompanied her. As this fellow waited in the corridor on a chair outside the door of the suite, Charley ushered Yiniang and Xiaoming in.

On the street, Charley would have passed them by, but here he recognized Yiniang the instant he saw her. She was of course older; time had coarsened her delicate features. Xiaoming's prominent eyes also rendered him easily recognizable.

Both of them were wearing the ubiquitous Mao suit, that high-collar, button-up, pseudo-military uniform that the Chairman was so fond of sporting and that everyone in the country—a billion souls, mind you—had to wear to demonstrate their allegiance. Now in 1978, a full two years after Mao's passing, people still didn't dare to venture out into the street in anything but a Mao suit. Charley remembered Yiniang used to be very fashionable, like our mother, but in a Mao suit she looked harsh and—common.

More disconcerting were Yiniang and Xiaoming's expressions—totally blank—as if they were wearing masks, but with a strong sense of fear and suspicion lurking behind. Neither showed any signs of recognition. When he invited them to sit down they sat at the edge of their chairs, as if prepared to make a quick getaway. They didn't touch the tea he poured for them. They didn't utter a word, not even a cursory greeting.

"Yiniang, you may not recognize me," my brother began, sensing that it was incumbent upon him to break the ice, "but I'm your nephew—you used to call me Charley. My mother is Dai Shangying, my father Liu Yongchio. I have two younger sisters, and we went to Taiwan..."

He stopped. What he just said had brought no reaction from them. They continued to treat him like a total stranger. He was surprised and at a loss, remembering how he, as a toddler in his first suit and tie, had proudly served as the ring-bearer at her wedding; how he hoped to stay with Yiniang when our mother kicked us out of the house one evening for being too rowdy and incurring the ire of our White Russian landlord. Had she forgotten him?

But how could he blame her? It was terrifying enough, he knew, that the Shanghai authorities had summoned her, that someone in an American official delegation wished to see her. Americans had long been branded as *evil imperialist-capitalists*. It was catastrophic for anyone to be remotely associated with them. For all she knew, it could be a trick to get her to confess yet another crime she hadn't committed.

My brother knew he had to take a different tack.

"You probably remembered 'Charley' as a skinny little boy wearing glasses, not this middle-aged man without glasses. I'm wearing contact lenses," he tried, getting nowhere.

In desperation my brother started to confess. "When I was a little boy, I was very naughty. One time I plucked all the camellia buds and flowers in a flower pot on your second story window ledge."

She was listening, without emotion.

"And I once urinated on the coal stove in your kitchen because I liked the hissing sound it made."

At that, Yiniang burst out crying. With her tears, she poured out, bit by painful bit, what had happened to them in the last 30 years.

Yiniang's husband—Shushu

Yiniang's husband, whom we called Shushu (Younger Paternal Uncle), was a gentle, quiet, and physically fragile man. To use a Chinese expression, his hands didn't have enough strength to tie up a chicken. He was the last relative we had seen before boarding our flight to Taiwan that predawn morning in Shanghai.

Desperate to persuade Shushu and family to leave, our father had even found a job for him as an attorney for the predecessor of China Air Lines in Taiwan.

To understand what happened to Shushu, we have to know about the Three-Anti and Five-Anti Campaigns launched by Mao in 1951 and 1952 respectively, a short two years after the founding of the People's Republic of China. The Three-Anti Campaign was against corruption, waste, and bureaucracy; Five-Anti was against bribery, theft of national property, tax evasion, cheating on government contracts, and stealing national economic information. On the surface they were all reasonable, legitimate, righteous aims. Who wouldn't want to be anti-corruption, for instance? But with tens of thousands of cadres, trained workers, propagandists, and anti-capitalist activists suddenly materializing and going door to door to spy and report on suspected offenders in large cities, anyone could be accused of one of the crimes and be branded as *an enemy of the state*.

As an attorney with a private practice and expertise in patent law, Shushu did not fit any of the eight categories. But because of his expertise in patent law, he had worked with an American law firm. His history of working with the *American imperialist-capitalists*—the two always went together, like conjoined twins—made him an *American imperialist-capitalist running dog.* And, by extension, an enemy of the state.

He was sent to a labor camp in Jiangxi province and died soon after. Yiniang never found out when or how he died and never saw his body. (Now we know that brutal torture was often involved, and that the campaigns led to hundreds of thousands of suicides—not all voluntary.) She could only be sure of one thing: he had not been shot, for if he had, she would have received a bill for the bullet.

Mother and Yiniang's Cousin—Our Seventh Uncle

Both Three-Anti and Five-Anti Campaigns were designed to root out political opponents—dissidents and potential dissidents—but the Five-Anti also amounted to an all-out war against the capitalists, the bourgeoisie. Mao even set a quota: "We must probably execute 10,000 to several tens of thousands of embezzlers nationwide before we can solve the problem."

Our Seventh Uncle, Mother and Yiniang's cousin, mentioned in the previous chapter, was an early victim. He was the relative who owned the resort in Lu Shan that my mother rushed home from as Nainai lay dying—Lu Shan, the fabled mountain where Chiang Kai-shek and later Mao Zedong spent their summers. He was doubtlessly the richest member of our extended family. Every year he engaged not one, but two of the most renowned Chinese opera troupes to perform at his house in Shanghai for his mother's birthday. As a child, I had once wandered into the opium den in his house in Shanghai during one of their lavish celebrations.

As mentioned in the previous chapter, Seventh Uncle had made a trip to Taiwan—most likely at my father's urging—before the "liberation" of the mainland, but decided against moving there. The island was too backward for him. The houses didn't have flush toilets. He was older—in his 50s—and he was fat; how could he be expected to squat over a stinky hole to go to the bathroom? And why should he? Unfortunately, he was just the kind of person the Communists wanted to eliminate.

The government seized all his property—companies, factories, houses and summer resort, and put him and his sons in jail. He committed suicide, and one son died in prison.

Our Maternal Grandmother—Wainainai

Although my mother was *the* most stoic person I have ever known, she expressed regret several times that she didn't succeed in persuading her mother to leave with us for Taiwan. Instead, Wainainai went to Shanghai to stay with Yiniang, her youngest daughter. Yiniang told my brother that Wainainai suffered a stroke in 1966, and was paralyzed for 10 years before passing away in 1976, two years previously, at age 96.

Those ten years coincided with the most tumultuous period in the Communist rule—the Great Proletarian Cultural Revolution. So Yiniang had nursed a bedridden mother during the decade when young Red Guards stormed every household. They forced everyone, including the aged and infirm, to perform the dedication dance to demonstrate allegiance to the Great Chairman Mao. Anyone who failed to perform to the Guards' satisfaction was brutally beaten.

When Yiniang recapitulated her life of the past 30 years for my brother that night, including Wainainai's stroke and death, she made no mention of the Cultural Revolution, its particulars, or her own sufferings. She spoke not a word of anger against the government or her sadistic young tormenters. Was it fear that the suite might have been bugged (very likely), concern that the cadre outside the door might be listening, or her true acceptance of all that had befallen her? Her account consisted of only bare-bone facts, and my brother asked no questions.

Yiniang and Shushu's Children—Our Four Cousins

Of Yiniang and Shushu's four children, our four cousins, it was sad to see how their fate had diverged from ours. Because their father was branded as an *an American imperialist-capitalist running dog* early on in the regime and their mother had *overseas connections*, the family was classified as one of the *Black Five Kinds*, the lowest of the low. The middle two children came of age at the worst time, when education was out of the question. The second child, Xiaodi, a girl, saw no future in Shanghai and decided to volunteer to go to the countryside. For a girl from Shanghai, the most cosmopolitan city in the country, to go to the countryside to work side by side with farmers was considered a fate second only to death. She married a fellow young exile, an overseas Chinese from Thailand. The third, Xiaoming, the only son, the one who accompanied Yiniang to the guesthouse to meet with my brother, became a factory worker. But his oldest sister, Xiaowei, somehow managed to attend Fudan University during politically more lenient times and became a mathematics professor. The youngest, Xiaochun (in the photo), studied chemical engineering and worked in a chemical factory in the province of Canton. They were all alive and married.

The Third Uncle—San Jiu

Our San Jiu, our third maternal uncle and his wife—the woman who had used Cousin Li so cruelly and didn't treat Wainainai, her mother-in-law, that well either—were still living in faraway Gansu, where they had settled during the Sino-Japanese war.

The Sixth Uncle—Liu Jiu

I recently saw a movie preview where a comment on the screen caught my eye: *Our lives are defined by moments, especially those we don't see coming.* I have never met my Sixth Uncle or seen a photo of him, the youngest of my mother's siblings. But I know one thing about him; I know the defining moment of his life.

He was in the volunteer Youth Army during the war against the Japanese and after the war lost no time in resuming his education at Qinghua University—one of the two top universities in China. A brilliant student about to graduate with a degree in physics, he was called to the office of his department head one day.

"I just got a letter from the university in Taiwan," the elderly professor informed Liu Jiu. The professor was obviously pleased about the news. "They are trying to build up their physics department and need a teaching assistant. I thought you would be a great fit. This is a job that offers excellent opportunities, because they can really use some good physicists."

Was my uncle hoping for a job from a better university? This must have been late spring 1948, before the civil war took a decisive turn for the worse for the Nationalists. He had never thought about going to Taiwan. To most Chinese, Taiwan was a painful reminder of one of the most humiliating pages in Chinese history because it became a Japanese colony after we lost the first Sino-Japanese war in 1895. A tiny island across the Taiwan Strait, it was only given back to us 50 years later when Japan surrendered in 1945. Every Chinese hated the Japanese, especially after the atrocities they committed during the war. Living in a former Japanese colony and working for an unknown university certainly did not appeal to my uncle. More importantly, he was tired of moving because of the war; he hadn't seen any of his family for years; he wanted to settle down and take care of his mother.

He turned down the position.

A classmate of his happened to be there too. This fellow was quick to seize the opportunity.

Their respective fates were sealed in that moment. I don't know who my uncle's friend was, but I know he later must have thanked his lucky stars that he grabbed this chance. Hindsight tells us that with the sudden influx of talents due to the fall of mainland, the obscure National Taiwan University quickly became one of the best higher educational institutions in Asia. In all likelihood my Sixth Uncle would have done very well at the university.

As a writer, I love to rewrite, changing a phrase here, embellishing a sentence there, and, for fiction, adding a twist somewhere, until the final copy is polished to my satisfaction. In my old age, however, I have come to realize that life itself is nothing but a rough draft. One comes to situations often unprepared, without the benefit of foresight. And life can be unforgiving. The choices we make are often irreversible. My mother, in her old age, ended my Sixth Uncle's story with a deep sigh. He was her youngest sibling, the baby of the family. Owing to the wars, I don't even know what he looks like, but I can never forget the choice he made that day. I don't know how and what he suffered due to his *overseas connection* "crime." During the height of Cultural Revolution, people were jumping off tall buildings like *xia jiaoze*—dropping meat dumplings in the pot—according to an eyewitness' vivid account. My uncle survived, but did he ever think about that fateful day and wonder *what if* he had made a different choice? Did he have regrets?

All we found out from Yiniang was that he taught physics at a high school in Suzhou and was married, with no children.

My brother talked with Yiniang for more than an hour that evening, exchanging information about who had died, who was where and doing what. No one on the Taiwan side had died. Charley told her about her two older brothers: our

Eldest Uncle, Da Jiu (cousin Li's father), and Fourth Uncle, Si Jiu. For all she knew, they had simply vanished, first Da Jiu, then later Si Jiu. She didn't know whether they had escaped or had been arrested and killed.

Yiniang hadn't expected us to survive, either. For many years the Communist government propaganda painted pictures of extreme deprivation in Taiwan, where people were reduced to eating banana peelings.

And the fear that evening was by no means on one side only. Afterward, my brother wrote home to our parents in Taiwan, judiciously omitting names, places, and details to avoid attracting attention of the letter censors, as Taiwan was still under martial law and the authorities took a dim view, to put it mildly, of anyone in touch with *Communist bandits*.

My father was equally circumspect. His letter showed no reaction, but in a visit to the States, he asked Charley, "Don't you think you were being rather reckless to set foot there?" Shouldn't he have been worried he'd be jailed—or worse?

With his childhood anecdotes, my brother managed to convince Yiniang that evening in 1978 that he really was her nephew. At first both sides treaded cautiously. We were afraid of endangering her and her family, and she, by force of past experience, was afraid of further calamities. Gradually the political situation relaxed; the Communist government became more open to the outside, so she no longer had to worry about getting into trouble. Still, in the end there proved to be more barriers between us that were far more difficult to overcome. In the end we failed our aunt; we failed in the areas where she most needed help.

However diligently we had followed news reports, we couldn't begin to fathom the lives of our relatives on the mainland during those 30 years, any more than they could conceive of our existence in the outside world. The whole Chinese mainland was literally locked up for 30 years, and its "inmates" were subjected to arbitrary, unthinkable cruelties in the form of torture, threats, coercions, humiliations, and fear—constant fear. Children were turned against parents, spouses against spouses, friends against friends. At the same time, they were told only what the government wanted them to know. The whole environment created a particular mind-set—either you were for Mao or against Mao, right or wrong—with no shades of gray in between.

When a billion people, each in a Mao suit, waved an identical little red book ("Quotations of Chairman Mao"), and hollered the same slogan "Long Live Chairman Mao" with equal fervor, something was terribly wrong.

When the emperor wore no clothes, people did not have the freedom to speak the truth. Worse, they had to speak the untruth and often bore false witness against themselves or someone else.

In short, for 30 years, our relatives on the mainland had lived in a vastly different world from ours.

Yiniang had a degree in accounting from Fudan University in Shanghai but had never worked a day outside her home until Shushu was sent to the labor camp to die. She managed to bring up four children and provide for Wainainai by working as an accountant. After we reconnected and the political situation eased some more, she told us she and Shushu had a savings account in an American bank holding more than $10,000. All those years, of course, she hadn't been able to touch a penny, couldn't even own up to having it. There it sat accruing interest, she thought, for almost 40 years. One day I received a carbon copy of one of the last letters sent by the bank, with the instruction from my parents to write to inquire about the account. I did but never received a reply. The bank might have moved, failed, or been bought by another bank. Maybe there was a statue of limitations regarding unclaimed bank deposits. In any case, her money was gone.

Yiniang had lived in the same three-story town home since she was married. The government decided early on that it was too big a place for her family and assigned a worker family to occupy the first floor. This was common practice. If one's living quarters were too large, one must have oppressed the proletarians. Now everyone should share and share alike. Unfortunately, the two families never got along; sometimes words were exchanged, which led to our cousin Xiaoming, whose health was delicate since childhood, getting beaten up. In desperation, Yiniang wrote to my brother and asked him to intervene by writing to the Chinese Vice Premier Li Xiannian, a traditional Chinese way of getting justice.

Through one of my father's friends in Shanghai who later moved to Beijing, she had heard that Charley, in the Bergland delegation in 1978, had met and shook hands with the Vice Premier. The truth was my brother was the lowest ranking member in the delegation. He had only been included at all because Bergland, at the last minute, realized they could use an ethnic Chinese in the group. My brother had no pull with Li Xiannian. Even if he did, it would have been highly inappropriate for him, as a civil servant of the American government, to write to the Chinese Vice Premier for any reason. There was nothing he could do to help Yiniang.

My parents were both 82 when they moved to the States to retire in 1989. Their departure from Taiwan helped Yiniang overcome her fear enough to propose a reunion with my mother in Hong Kong.

Alas, it was too late. My mother had suffered a severe heart attack in 1980, the result of decades of smoking—a legacy of the Sino-Japanese War, when a doctor advised her to take up smoking to reduce stress. Years of painful rheumatoid arthritis disabled her, while macular degeneration blinded her. Worst of all, her mind was robbed by Alzheimer' disease during the last ten years of her life. My father died at 87 in 1994 in Maryland, my mother at 91. She and Yiniang never reunited.

Such was the story of a family torn apart by the war—the war that brought on civil war and the ruthless Communist regime. Thomas Wolfe famously declared, "You can't go home again." These days my Chinese-American friends seem to be in the habit of visiting China for any reason at all. Some have even bought houses there. As for me, I left Shanghai more than 65 years ago on a February morning with weak legs and a joyous heart, without realizing that I would never go home again.

During my 50 plus years in this country, to the not-infrequent question, "But where are you *really* from?" I always gave my stock short answer: "I was born and raised in Shanghai."

Now, finally, I have a long answer—this book.

ACKNOWLEDGMENTS

When Dr. Barry Jacobs, clinical psychologist and family therapist, first saw me, I was a very depressed patient. With his extraordinary perception, intelligence, and empathy, he guided me—with subtle, sometimes not so subtle hints—to an emotional space in which I was able to write after a seven-year hiatus. Without him, this book would not have been possible.

I arrived in Pennsylvania on a Tuesday night in August 2008 and met Lynn DeMarco on Friday morning. She has been my first line of defense, good friend, and support ever since. Her energy work has given me a new lease on life each time and has made it possible for me to devote the hours necessary for writing.

Megan Webster is a well-known poet in San Diego, my former poetry teacher turned friend and editor, whose editing and suggestions were crucial in the initial shaping of this book.

Caught up in incredibly busy lives, my daughter, Andrea, and son, Clif, both served as first readers and all-around computer support. Then Andrea volunteered to do the second round of editing, reorganized some of the content and made pivotal suggestions. I'm also grateful to her for being the family historian, saving documents and photos that contributed greatly to this book. Thanks are also due to my son-in-law, Douglas Durian, whose expressed desire of wanting to read more gave me the impetus to share more of my past in this book. Kudos to my twelve-year-old granddaughter, Sylvia Durian, who took on the important task of converting all the photos electronically. All three read the manuscript and made suggestions.

Dante Fuoco, an English major and senior at Swarthmore College, was recommended to me as an editor by a professor of English at Swarthmore. Young enough to be my grandson, he was game enough to take on the challenge of this cross-generational and cross-cultural material. The combination of his writer's sensitivity, editor's good judgment and unfamiliarity with the history and culture of the period worked to my advantage. Since some of the content is painful for me to explore, his questions and comments challenged me to think deeper and further and improved the book immeasurably.

I'm forever in debt to Jeffrey Buczacki for doing the final read through of the manuscript and his wife, my dear writer friend Teresa, for volunteering him. Jeff is the truest Renaissance man I know. I would not have had the audacity to ask for his help, but once he did, I can't imagine what I would have done without it—his astute eye, impeccable taste in language, breadth and depth of knowledge, generous spirit, and expeditious input.

Last but not least, I wish to thank my brother Charley. Being three years older—or, as he would correct me, two years and five months older—he was privy to more information in the early years than I. This book owes a great deal to his remarkable memory. The hours we spent on the phone reminiscing about our shared past were the happiest for me during the long, lonely, and arduous writing process.

CPSIA information can be obtained at www.ICGtesting.com
Printed in the USA
LVOW121637281112

309224LV00001B/52/P